ME to WE

A Pastor's Discovery of the Power of Partnership

by Alan Nelson

Group

Loveland, Colorado
www.group.com

Group resources actually work!

This Group resource helps you focus on **"The 1 Thing®"**— a life-changing relationship with Jesus Christ. "The 1 Thing" incorporates our **R.E.A.L.** approach to ministry. It reinforces a growing friendship with Jesus, encourages long-term learning, and results in life transformation, because it's:

Relational
Learner-to-learner interaction enhances learning and builds Christian friendships.

Experiential
What learners experience through discussion and action sticks with them up to 9 times longer than what they simply hear or read.

Applicable
The aim of Christian education is to equip learners to be both hearers and doers of God's Word.

Learner-based
Learners understand and retain more when the learning process takes into consideration how they learn best.

Me to We: A Pastor's Discovery of the Power of Partnership

Copyright © 2007 Alan Nelson

Visit our Web site: **www.group.com**

Credits

Editor: Jim Watkins
Senior Developer: Roxanne Wieman
Project Manager: Scott Kinner
Chief Creative Officer: Joani Schultz
Copy Editor: Lidonna Beer
Art Director: Jeff Storm
Print Production Artist: Steven Plummer, Bethany Press
Cover Art Director/Designer: Jeff Storm
Illustrator(s): Steven Plummer, Bethany Press
Production Manager: DeAnne Lear

Unless otherwise noted, Scripture taken from the HOLY BIBLE, NEW INTERNATIONAL VERSION®. Copyright © 1973, 1978, 1984 by International Bible Society. Used by permission of Zondervan Publishing House. All rights reserved.

Library of Congress Cataloging-in-Publication Data
Nelson, Alan E.
Me to we : a pastor's discovery of the power of partnership / by Alan Nelson.
     p. cm.
ISBN 978-0-7644-3486-0
(pbk. : alk. paper) 1. Church renewal. 2. Church management. 3. Laity. I. Title.
  BV600.3.N45 2007
  253–dc22
                              2007029593
ISBN 978-0-7644-3486-0

10 9 8 7 6 5 4 3 2 1   16 15 14 13 12 11 10 09 08 07
Printed in the United States of America.

What Church Leaders Say About *Me to We*

"*Me to We* is a pronoun shift with deep theological implications. The vibrant, magnetic church that God had in mind emerges when the leadership focus is on equipping and developing God's people. His church was intended to be a reflection of the people and gifts that reside in it…this book can take us there."

—Nancy Ortberg, founding partner, Teamworx2, www.teamworx2.com

"One of the most unfortunate realities of ministry is the well-meaning but drained leader. Too many leaders think their responsibility is to take everything on themselves. But it's a mentality that has devastating effects both on the leader and the led. In his book, *Me to We*, Alan Nelson takes a unique look at the dual challenge of leading and equipping others to lead. No matter where you are in the ministry, this book will show you that the key to successful ministry isn't necessarily carrying everything on your own shoulders; it's learning to equip others to help."

—Ed Young, pastor of Fellowship Church; author, *The Creative Leader*

"A refreshing look at leadership that involves letting go of current models and embracing the ancient model of the early church—releasing laity in leveraged ministry ventures."

—Bob Buford, founding chairman, Leadership Network; author, *Halftime* and *Finishing Well*

"I love *Me to We*. *Me to We* is a must-read for any pastor or leader in the church who wants to see their local congregation move from just adding ministry to multiplying it. The principle of partnerships, which the book so brilliantly illustrates, is an essential concept that will be welcomed and appreciated by many overburdened, lonely pastors and leaders who find themselves weary in ministry. This book provides welcome relief and positive steps in the right direction."

—James C. Poit, executive pastor, Crystal Cathedral Ministries

"Alan Nelson is a seasoned pastor who 'gets' pastors and is an excellent coach of pastors. I've been learning from him for over a decade. In a creative and refreshing style, this book calls us back to recapture God's dream for team ministry."

—Gene Appel, lead pastor of Willow Creek Community Church

"Alan Nelson is a pastor of pastors. He has a unique way of challenging the way I think about church and helping me see leadership in a new light. A must-read for pastors who haven't figured everything out yet!"

—Mark Batterson, pastor of National Community Church

"What could be a more biblical model of ministry? Every pastor should read Alan Nelson's account of moving from the pastor-centric 'me' to the partnership-equipping 'we.' It will revolutionize the way you do ministry."

—Les Parrott III, Ph.D., founder of RealRelationships.com; author, *Relationships*

"The longer I have been in ministry, the longer I realize that if we in church leadership do not move from Me to We and heed to the philosophy of Ephesians 4, we will not be a healthy church and won't have healthy church leaders. This book gives great and very practical guidance of how to go about shifting from a 'me' to a 'we' mentality in church leadership."

—Dan Kimball, pastor of Vintage Faith Church; author, *They Like Jesus but Not the Church*

"Alan Nelson knows how to mentor pastors and understands how to transfer his knowledge into one terrific book. This book will breathe life, encouragement, and restoration into the hearts of tired pastors everywhere. *Me to We* is destined to positively impact the church world!"

—Stan Toler, author and pastor

"Pastors tell me that the lack of 'mobilized and motivated laity' is their greatest frustration in ministry. Finally a book that tells us how to solve the problem! Alan Nelson and *Me to We* solve one of the greatest 'growth-restricting obstacles' churches face today—overworked pastors and under-mobilized laity."

—Chip Arn, Church Growth Institute

"So many pastors neglect their calling to make disciples, instead keeping too busy with remedial tasks. Alan Nelson has succeeded in creating an interesting dialogue between two pastors that describes this struggle. This book is an excellent help to any pastor who wants to figure out how to begin to follow the Ephesians 4 command of equipping believers for the work of the ministry."

—Ed Stetzer, co-author of *Comeback Churches: How 300 Churches Turned Around and Yours Can Too*

"*Me to We* nails it! Leadership is a team sport and must be shared if you want to chase ministry dreams during the day, and still sleep well at night! Read it and rediscover the joy!"

—H. Dale Burke, pastor of First Evangelical Free Church of Fullerton; author, *How to Lead and Still Have a Life*

"Alan is one of the best at defining the role of the pastor as a vision womb who helps connect people to their God-wired destiny. His clarity on defining the distinctions between equipping, developing, and training is excellent!"

—Mike Slaughter, pastor of Ginghamsburg Church

"This book reads like a screenplay; in fact, just take it to church, assign your actors, and teach/train the entire congregation to learn the secret of *Me to We* ministry in a single evening!"

—Becky Tirabassi, speaker; author, *Sacred Obsession*

"This is one of the best books I've read in a long time. Too many leaders think that one more program, or one more staff member, will solve the problem of disengaged people. And ironically, pastors create their own roadblocks by holding on to that which they wish to give away: the ministry itself. This book helps pastors face the necessary personal changes that must be made in order to give the ministry away."

—Kevin Ford, chief visionary officer/managing partner of TAG

"Alan Nelson is one of my favorite authors. In *Me to We*, he has written an engaging book concerning a critical topic. It's a must-read for any leader struggling to do all that is demanded of him or her."

—Steve Stroope, senior pastor of Lake Pointe Church

"This book is much more than just another book about volunteerism—it is an entire philosophy of ministry development and leadership. It is compelling and significant. This is the church as it was meant to be."

—Tammy Kelley, executive director of strategic implementation at Willow Creek Community Church

"*Me to We* is of great importance. The future of the church is, as it has always been, in the hands of the people. Alan Nelson's call fits into the priesthood of all believers chorus that has been sung throughout the ages. This book is not only a call for a new way to be the church, it provides a plan for a way forward—this book may well be a crucial element in helping churches build on their greatest strengths—their people led by the spirit of God."

—Doug Pagitt, pastor of Solomon's Porch

"This book is an easy, quick read that kept my interest and offers many gems of wisdom for pastors who want an equipping congregation that actually deploys its people for service. I can't wait to put this book in the hands of traditional pastors seeking a new fruitfulness in their own lives and among the people of their congregations."

—E. Stanley Ott, Ph.D., president of the Vital Churches Institute

"A cross between *Tuesdays With Morrie* and *The Five Dysfunctions of a Team*, Alan's book reads easily and lands solidly. It's a must-read for any pastor who is serious about growing a healthy church where God's people are empowered to be what God intended them to be. It is packed with practical principles that will help you take your church to the next level."

—Dan Reiland, executive pastor of Crossroads Community Church

"Hey, I got an idea. To get a congregation in shape, let's have the pastor diet, do sit-ups, and run laps for all of us. Surely, that will make us all healthier. Right? Not! Yet this off-the-wall scenario is actually being played out each week in many congregations. A better and more biblical approach engages the whole body of Christ using their giftedness to minister to one another. Alan Nelson unpacks how to make this become reality in one's own church."

—John R. Cionca, Bethel Seminary; author, *Inviting Volunteers to Minister*

"I'm convinced that to reverse the church's current declining direction in North America, the church of the 21st century will have to address no less than three major issues, one of which is empowering pastors and staff to equip and release their people to do Great Commission ministry. If you're a pastor or active in your church, you need to read this book!"

—Aubrey Malphurs, lead navigator of the Malphurs Group; senior professor of pastoral ministries at Dallas Seminary

"Alan Nelson gives us a clear and compelling roadmap for how to do this every day in the churches we serve. For those of us who know that if we could just 'let go more,' then God would be able to work more, this is our book!"

—Nelson Searcy, lead pastor of The Journey Church of the City; founder, www.ChurchLeaderInsights.com

"Get ready to be challenged! Although written as a conversation, this book is full of great practical insights to build and strengthen you and your church. Challenge yourself to become a *Me to We* leader."

—Erik Rees, Saddleback ministry director; author, *S.H.A.P.E.: Finding and Fulfilling Your Unique Purpose for Life*

Dedication

This book is dedicated to the visionaries and catalysts of the contemporary, equipping emphasis, such as Bob Buford, Jim Garlow, Greg Ogden, Wayne Cordiero, Tammy Kelley, Chris Hardy, Don Simmons, Brad Smith, and the spark plug of the movement, Sue Mallory.

Table of Contents

Thanks

This project lived up to its content, meaning it was a group task. It wasn't just me coming up with ideas and cooking solo in the privacy of my literary kitchen. Thanks goes to Joani Schultz, Vernon Armitage, Robie Sullivan, Don Miller, Sue Mallory, Chris Hardy, and my sweetheart, Nancy Nelson, for their sometimes painful but constructive edits, ideas, critiques, and improvements that made this book far better than it would have been otherwise. Teams sometimes aren't efficient, but they're usually more effective.

Thanks also to my colleagues: Karl Leuthauser, Roxy Wieman, Jeff Storm, and Craig Cable. Ministry Essentials rocks! Jim Watkins, I appreciate you smoothing out the conversations in this narrative; you're awesome. Cary Dunlap, thanks for your work on getting the Web site items in place. The Rev! Magazine team is also incredible, for morphing Rev! into America's only pastors magazine committed primarily to helping pastors multiply their ministries through the equipping value.

See, even small things like a book, have a lot of people involved. How much more do we need our local churches, small or large, to function like vibrant, dynamic, multifaceted organizations that synergize each other's strengths for maximum impact? I believe this is the only way we can grow people and impact our communities for Christ.

—Alan Nelson

Introduction

Something happens to a person at midlife. Psychologists suggest our reference point changes from how many years we've lived to how many years we have left. It's time's equivalent to the continental divide in topography. You begin to analyze life and what you do at a deeper level. If your first half has been less productive than you dreamed, you begin poking and prodding status quo, wondering if there might be something more effective that you missed in the first round. My dad says that life is like a roll of toilet paper. The less you have left, the faster it goes. Mess with the metaphor all you want, but the heart of this book is about striving to make a difference with the remaining sheets on my roll.

After two decades of church planting and connecting with seekers and those disenchanted with church life, I had the opportunity to become a part of Group Publishing. As the executive editor of Rev! Magazine, I am privileged to champion pastoral ministry in and through this great organization. While interacting with hundreds and observing tens of thousands of churches across the country from many tribes, I've had an opportunity to meet some extremely effective pastors and congregations. They are a unique but growing segment of pastors and churches. They've discovered what it takes to catalyze spiritual growth and effective service beyond church walls—minus the burnout of those pastors who lead them.

These unique congregations have inspired this book. We're driving a stake in the ground, believing there is a better way to "do" church. The journey begins with the pastors changing the way they think about their role and how it is carried out. This book will rub some people the wrong way. No one likes to be told that what they've invested in is misaligned. Yet, most pastors realize that the results they're seeing in their church are less than they desire. In spite of better education, ministry resources, and as many books and conferences as a person can ingest, few churches significantly impact their surrounding communities.

This book is joining a family of resources created originally by Leadership Network and then acquired by Group to coincide with what has become the largest volunteer membership association in the country: Church Volunteer Central, which is approaching 10,000 members in only its third year! But don't let the name deceive you. This is not about gaining more "cheap laborers" for the kingdom. Volunteer is a cultural, not a biblical term. Rather, this is about empowering the multiplicity of

God-given gifts in every congregation. This is about doing church differently, so we can actualize our potential of impacting lives inside and outside the ecclesiastical walls. Our vision is to fan the flames of what God is already doing through a growing number of externally focused churches, lay-mobilized congregations, and truly team-oriented ministries.

+ + +

Jesus used the power of parable to engage listeners and provide key insights into his kingdom. Even though I'm not much of a fiction reader—preferring a nonfiction book any time to a sugary romance or intriguing mystery—there is something that happens in a fable or story that can't occur in a traditional nonfiction book. Our lives are basically values and concepts that become incarnate through conversations, decisions, and—in the arena of the church—ministry and events. I've personally been touched by contemporary storytellers such as Og Mandino, Ken Blanchard, Spencer Johnson, and Patrick Lencioni. Whether you're a fiction fan or a nonfiction reader, I hope you'll enjoy the format and content of this book.

Me to We is based on real people, whose churches have become bold, dynamic congregations. A variety of pastors and church staff collaborated in the process, so that the conversations reflect the journeys of those who've transformed their congregations dynamically. This was a team process. We are convinced that your church has what it takes to reach its potential. But chances are if you're following the traditional model of pastoring in America, it will never reach that potential, regardless of its size. Our prayer is that by the end of this book, you'll be inspired to pursue a different way of doing what God called you to do as pastor.

THE
PAIN

The meeting

weary in well Doing

The first step

unpacking at Home

After several minutes of futile attempts to pray, Pastor Matt Robinson lifted his head from his hands. Lately, it seemed like the noise in his head drowned out his quiet time. As soon as he closed his eyes, his mind raced to church matters. Whether it was Earl in the hospital, the heated debate in the parking lot after the church board meeting, the empty ministry positions, the tight finances, or the complaints of the older members about the music, his desire to focus on God's face faded in light of these pressing ministry needs. And yet, amid his busy thoughts, the early morning solitude of his study felt like a refuge from the endless stream of tasks that awaited his weekly schedule at church.

What frustrated Matt the most was that in spite of his 24/7 availability and long hours of ministry, the congregation seemed stuck. They weren't growing like he'd hoped during his three years in this new position. Even with their minimal increase in attendance the last couple of years, the taxing schedule of meetings, tight finances, and seemingly marginal commitment among church attendees left him exhausted. His wife, Carmen, and their two kids were very patient, even though it seemed he'd spent little quality time with them. Although he never admitted it openly, he'd begun to doubt if he were really cut out for the ministry. He loved teaching, preaching, and interacting with people; but so many of the administrative, staffing, and organizational activities daily depleted his joy.

Matt looked at the stack of mail and papers on his desk. Desiring to avoid the mess, he decided to concentrate on his sermon prep. He grabbed his laptop and headed out the office door. Starbucks was only a few blocks down the street. He hopped in his car and drove toward the familiar green logo. After mixing three Splendas and some half-and-half into his grande coffee, he looked over the crowd of commuters, searching to find a place to work on his message.

He noticed someone he recognized. There in the corner sat Vernon Miller, an older man who pastored Westover Church, a growing congregation here in Pleasant Valley. Pastor Miller had a stack of books in front of him, his attention focused on a legal pad of paper. Matt had never visited Westover, but he was constantly hearing about it in the newspaper and community grapevine. He'd even lost some of his members to it. Vernon had stopped in to welcome Matt when he first arrived. He'd seen him a time or two at community events.

At first Matt hesitated bothering him. *Sometimes I don't like being interrupted when I'm working on a message*, Matt thought. *He's probably forgotten who I am. We're just a little church in Westover's shadow.*

In spite of Matt's reservations, Vernon's mild demeanor seemed unassuming, so he changed directions and walked toward the pastor. *I'll just say hi*, Matt thought.

Pastor Matt walked to Vernon's table. The gray-haired man, sensing someone standing nearby, looked up from his yellow legal pad, a smile already on his face. "Hi, sorry to bother you, but I'm Matt Robinson, pastor down at Crossroads," Matt said.

The elder preacher immediately stood and extended his hand. "Well, sure you are. Good to see you again. Vernon Miller, Westover Church," he responded, shaking hands with Matt.

"I didn't want to interrupt you; just wanted to say hi."

"Oh, no problem," the older pastor said, moving his books and papers to one corner of the small table. "Have a seat in my office. I've been thinking of calling you lately."

"I know you're busy. Are you sure?"

"Absolutely," Vernon responded, sitting down and patting the table, as if assuming Matt would join him. "You know, it's a sin the way we pastors get so consumed in our ministries that we don't take the time out to connect more. But you know, I pray for you at least once a week when I drive by your church on my way to the office. Really, have a seat, I'd love to get to know you better."

Vernon seemed genuinely interested in Matt. In spite of the pressure Matt felt to get his own work done, the morning's weariness motivated him to take up Vernon on his offer. "I'll only take a few minutes of your time," Matt said, putting his cup on the table and leaning his computer bag on the chair beside him.

"So how goes the battle?" Vernon asked, looking intently into the younger pastor's eyes.

For an instant, Matt considered responding with the typical pastoral response when asked "How are things going?" but the heaviness of his heart and the genuine look on Vernon's face encouraged him to let down his guard.

"Well, to be honest," Matt said, pausing for a last chance to change his mind, "not too well."

"Why is that?"

"I don't know. Maybe you can tell me. I'm putting in 50 to 60 hours a week, doing my best to serve people, but it never seems enough. I can't get ahead, and our church just doesn't seem to be growing much."

The older man leaned back in his chair. "Tell me more."

"Well, I'm not sure what more there is to say. I mean, I'm going sunup to sundown, juggling all these balls…like meetings, hospital visits, e-mails, phone calls, preparing for the Sunday message, or doing who knows how many other tasks it takes to keep our church running. Sometimes I just wonder if it's all worth it. I suppose Westover is big enough to have a staff that does everything."

Vernon laughed. "Sorry, you remind me of me. Years ago, I felt the same thing. I used to go to all these pastor conferences and read the latest ministry books. I was convinced that if I could just become like one of the guys teaching, I'd have it made."

"You do, don't you?" Matt asked, smiling big as if waiting for his friend to acknowledge what he sensed.

"Yes, I actually do, but not because of how you think." Vernon paused. "Westover has become a dream place for me to pastor. I don't deserve it. But it didn't get that way through conventional means. It's been quite a journey."

"Well, I'm game to learn," Matt said, taking a sip of his coffee and leaning back, expecting some pat answers or conceptual clichés.

"Are you?"

Matt waited before responding—something in the way the old man asked the question made him think it wasn't rhetorical. Matt paused a moment, feeling the pressure of his tear ducts filling. "I think I am," he said quietly, his throat constricted by emotions. "Things are turning out different than I'd hoped."

Weary in Well Doing

Vernon smiled reassuringly. "A few years ago I read a book called *Embracing Brokenness.** I forget the author's name, but it helped me during a really dark time in my life. I came to realize that in order for us leaders to develop as God wants, it usually requires a period of brokenness, when we embrace our own failures and inadequacies and then submit to God's renovating."

He stopped, waiting to see if Matt was tracking with him. Matt nodded thoughtfully.

Vernon continued, "I don't understand it. Maybe it's the curse of church work, but for some reason, what is happening inside a pastor has a direct impact on the church, more than any other organization. Before a church can change, the pastor must change…on the inside."

"What do you mean?"

"I mean there's a boatload of great ideas on how to improve a church, but for all practical purposes, they're meaningless until the pastor is willing to look inside first. We keep thinking the answer is 'out there' in some other church or book or great model. Sometimes it is. But like the parable of the soils, unless there is fertile ground in which to fall, the seed of even a great idea won't take root."

"So you mean it's about prayer and all that?"

"Well, prayer is certainly part of that, but chances are you've already been praying."

Matt nodded. "Trying to," he mumbled.

"It's almost more of a surrendering. You've got to realize that you don't have what it takes to help your church reach its potential or even to just get to the next level—so that you have to reinvent yourself before you try to change the church."

"Hmm?" Matt stared at his coffee. "I feel like my heart's right with God."

"It's not so much a matter of rightness as it is a willingness to embrace something so different that you can't stay the same; that you allow God to change how you think about yourself and your ministry. You've got to do that before you ever try and figure out what or how your church needs to change. In other words, until you get to a place where you're willing to retool who you are, chances are slim that anything I tell you will make a significant difference." Vernon took a drink from his coffee.

"So it's about me."

"In one way, it really *is* about you. At least that's where you have to start, because you're the pastor of your church. God has called you to shepherd your congregation, which means what happens in you will be significant to those you influence."

"I think I see. So where do I start?"

"Well, let's start with the pain points. If you need to change first in order for your congregation to grasp what it must do—and since most change is motivated by pain—explain why it's uncomfortable to stay where you're at."

"Well, like I said, I believe I'm called and I love my position, but I'm frustrated by the lack of progress."

"Like what? Give me examples."

Matt chuckled cynically. "Where do I start? OK, I work my brains out creating interesting messages and delivering them well, but month after month, it seems that people don't grow much. We've got people who have been coming to church their entire lives and I've yet to see the fruit of the Spirit in them. Some of them are judgmental of those who are different from them and sometimes critical of the way I lead. Yet they think they're saints because they've been Christians most of their lives. I've got some high-octane business people who—and I can see it in their eyes—just don't think I know how to lead. Maybe I don't, but I'm afraid if I let them have power, they'd try to take over the church. I feel badly about it, but it's my job to be in charge, isn't it?"

"Is it?"

Matt paused, thinking he might be walking into a trap. "Well, that's what I've been taught."

"I think you're in charge...to charge up others and then turn them loose. We'll talk about that later. So what else disappoints you about your ministry?"

"I feel like I'm always on call: running to the hospital, visiting some of the older members, trying to be at birthday parties, graduations, and meetings; besides prepping for weddings, funerals, and the like. Since everyone works during the day, about the only time I have to meet with them is at night, which takes away from my family time. I can't remember when my wife and I had a date."

"All right, what else?"

Matt laughed. "Isn't that enough? You're enjoying this, aren't you?"

Vernon returned the laugh. "Nope; just been there, done that, bought the T-shirt."

"OK, so while I'm complaining, let's talk about the lack of involvement. We've got the typical 20 percent of people doing 80 percent of the work. I'm tired of trying to recruit people to teach Sunday school or serve on the board or run the sound. We've had slots open in our church office, youth department, and children's ministry for a long time. We guilt someone into helping, turn around, and find that someone else has quit on us. People are so busy anymore that it's hard for them to do more than attend Sunday mornings a couple of times a month."

"OK, what else?"

"OK, you asked for it. Money! We'd love to hire staff to run some of the ministries, but even with our modest growth the last couple of years, we're not close to being able to bring on the two people we'd like to head up our youth and worship ministries. Since these programs aren't strong, we have a hard time attracting people who would help pay for this, so it's the old Catch-22 thing. I don't know why, but our people just aren't strong givers, in spite of the periodic pledge drive or stewardship message."

"Is that all?"

"Good night, man! Aren't you depressed yet? You're probably glad you're not pastoring my church."

"I used to pastor that kind of church. That's what Westover was like. And it's nothing I haven't heard a thousand times from other pastors. What else?"

"Well, I'm doing more and more things I just don't enjoy. If you told me I'd be doing the amount of administrative and caregiving things I am, I don't know if I'd have signed up for the job. I feel like the ministry is sucking all the joy out of me, which doesn't always make me the easiest guy to live with at home. I haven't exercised in who knows how long, and I feel like I can never get ahead. I…" Matt stopped. He quickly looked away from Vernon and out the window, tears welling up in his eyes.

Embracing Brokenness, by Alan Nelson (NavPress, 2002)

The First Step

Matt composed himself. "Sorry. I guess I've been keeping a lot in."

"No problem. Like I said, you sound like me several years ago. I felt like I was doing all the right things. In fact, Westover was growing, but I was killing myself in the process. We didn't have the commitment or the spiritual growth I was expecting; and for some reason, if I was being honest with myself, I wasn't enjoying the ministry much anymore."

"So what did you do?"

"I did what you're doing now: taking an inventory of what I didn't like. But first I did a lot of looking...out there," he waved his hand away from him. "I thought the answer resided somewhere in a great program or ministry model that I hadn't yet discovered."

"You mean it doesn't?" Matt said loudly and laughed.

"Well, it's out there, I think, but it has to start in here," Vernon said, patting his heart. "Whenever a church gets stuck, leaders need to change something about who they are or how they think about themselves and their role. Until that happens, the church won't get to the next level. That's the hardest work, letting go of our own security and self-image issues."

"Like what?"

"I can't tell you for sure. Chances are yours are different than mine were, but we all have a sense of who we should be as a pastor and what we're to do. We tend to think that the reason things aren't going better in our church is because of our people or our tradition or any number of other things. Some people give up the ministry because they just feel inferior, but that's usually not it."

"Yeah, sounds like the guy who went to his therapist and the counselor said, 'You don't have an inferiority complex. You really are inferior.'"

The two men laughed, then Vernon continued.

"I guess what I'm trying to say is that the first step toward change is a truly humble heart. That's the prerequisite for being teachable. You come to a place in your life and ministry when you begin to embrace the change that you desire in others or your church. You ever read Jim Collins?"

"Sure, *Good to Great?*"

"Yeah, that's the one. Collins says that one of the things common among organizations, both in the corporate realm as well as the social sector, is that they almost always have what he calls a fifth-level leader, someone who tends to be humble, strong, and frequently behind the scenes."

"That doesn't sound like a lot of the great pastors you hear about."

"Yeah, I know what you mean. I'm no judge of motive or character, but my gut tells me that the more we come to the realization that it's not about us, we gain a perspective that can truly take our churches from good to great."

"So it's about us, but it's not about us."

"Yup. Church change begins with the pastor embracing brokenness, and giving up some of the beliefs and self-image issues that get telegraphed to the church and its various ministries. My brokenness came because I was desperate for the congregation I was serving to become strong and healthy, but no matter how much I worked, it just didn't seem to be working."

"I thought you said that Westover was growing?"

"You know, years ago I gave up on the idea that people attending is a sign of spiritual growth, just as remaining small is not an indicator of holiness. McDonald's is popular, but you can't convince me they have the best food."

"True," Matt said, stirring his coffee as Vernon continued.

"I have no doubt that most of us in ministry are well-intended. I do think that most of us, by nature, get caught up in a codependent relationship with our congregations. We perform ministry services for them, which they applaud, so we do more. But all the while, we're creating a dependent relationship, so that our parishioners never really mature spiritually. They become spiritual consumers, full of knowledge but light on application. We beat them up with a few sermons here and there that don't seem to work. Then they beat us up with criticism here and there or pull out altogether. We scratch our heads and wonder: Is this what church is all about? I came to the conclusion that there must be a better way to develop people and not lose my own soul in the process."

"I always thought that if we could just grow enough to hire staff, then we could keep growing and I wouldn't have to kill myself in the process."

"The staff carrot is a tempting one to pursue. But the church ministry culture pretty much attracts those who think like we think, that if we just do enough ministry, we'll grow people. We see an occasional victory or bright spot, so we assume it's just hard work—that we're on the right track. But more pastoral staff just means more codependent relations—in the traditional mode, that is. If you get inside the typical megachurch, what you'll find is a lot of tired, overworked staff feeling the pressure to perform a little bit better. Sound familiar? What is true for pastors is also true for staff members."

Matt sat, thinking about what Vernon had said.

Vernon broke the silence. "Brother, if you want to meet, I'd be happy to share with you what I've learned, but it's up to you. No pressure."

"That sounds great," Matt said. "I'd really appreciate it. Will it be awkward that our churches are in the same community?"

Vernon smiled. "It won't be strange for me if it's not for you. We've got so many needs in Pleasant Valley that there are more than enough opportunities for churches like ours. My sense is that God isn't redundant. He's got exciting plans for Crossroads just as he has a unique blueprint for Westover. When we help each other, the kingdom gets better for everyone."

"OK, it's a deal," Matt said, extending his hand. "I really appreciate your willingness to meet with me today. Sorry to interrupt your work."

"No problem. Must have been a God thing. Let's set up a meeting in a week or two and we'll unpack this further. Have a great week."

*Unpacking
at Home*

When Matt went home that day, he told his wife about running into Vernon and the ensuing conversation.

"Do you buy into this idea?" Carmen asked. "It sounds like a lot of things would have to change around Crossroads for that to happen."

"I'm not sure what I think," Matt admitted. "But if it can help our church get out of its holding pattern and help me do more of what I feel called to do and what I'm good at, then I'm willing to take a closer look. What do you think?"

Carmen paused. "I agree. I also think that your family needs you right now. The kids are young. Anything that can improve that part of our lives, I'm all for it. I don't like the way we're living lately, always running here and there and having so many meetings at night. It doesn't make sense that a pastor should have to sacrifice his own family to serve people who often don't realize or appreciate all that you do."

"Carmen, we've talked about this before. I'm doing the best I can."

"I know. I'm just saying that we can't go on like this. I don't want our kids to grow up blaming God for not letting their dad be with them because he was always out serving the church."

"I know, I know. There's got to be a better way. I always thought that if we could get more staff, then we'd be able to cover the bases, but Vernon seems to imply that isn't the answer either."

"Probably not, because then you'd just burnout the staff. It's just more of the same. You know what it was like when you were on staff at First Church. They were never satisfied with what was happening and always pushing for more."

"I know. Plus, Vernon really got me thinking about this…but it just seems like we'll never see our people mature spiritually until more of them take ownership of the ministry. That's why we got into the ministry to begin with. To be honest, I'm pretty excited about having a new approach."

"I can see that—you haven't been this excited in a long time. And it does seem to make sense. But how do you do it? That's what I'm curious about."

"Me too. I guess that's what I have to learn next. We agreed to meet again in a couple weeks. He gave me a couple books to begin reading, so I can get started."

principle

People rarely change until there
is significant pain or discomfort
with the way things are.

the
PRICE

"in"ventory

a new baler

it's not your church

but wait, there's more

i'd get fired for that

losses

THE PRICE

"In"ventory

The two weeks until the next Starbucks meeting with Vernon flew by for Matt. Even though he felt a bit embarrassed by his emotional letdown in front of Vernon, his mind churned with curiosity as to where the elder pastor was going in their discussion. He said it wasn't something "out there" and yet was more than merely an internal change. Matt thought a lot about Vernon's statement that the congregation's journey for change starts with the pastor changing internally what he thinks and externally how he functions.

Matt felt the motivation to change his approach to ministry even more this week. They'd had an especially tense board meeting because of ongoing financial problems. It seemed as if they were constantly having to adjust the budgets, moving money from one account to another to cover the necessities, and were on the verge of laying off staff. He'd never admit it to anyone, but it felt good daydreaming about resigning from Crossroads. Maybe there was a better place for his gifts—a church where his long hours would yield more results. Maybe he should secretly send out a few résumés or check the minister-search Web sites.

Unfortunately the prolonged meetings had created even more tension at home, so that Matt's wife had finally had enough of his excuses about why he wasn't spending more time with the family. One night they had a veritable meltdown.

"Look, Matt," Carmen nearly shouted, hurling the dishcloth into the sink. "I have done everything I can do to support your ministry. But you said you'd be home at 8 to help with getting the kids ready for bed and to help with the dishes. Do you know what time it is, Matt?" Her voice had gone dangerously soft. "It's after 10." Matt could see in her eyes that tears were only moments away as she turned and walked quickly from the room.

He looked at his watch. 10:35 p.m. It was too late to call Vernon, he wasn't in the mood for TV, and the thought of working simply drained him. He sat heavily on the couch, head in his hands. *What am I going to have to do to get off this treadmill?* he thought. *How many people at the end of the week are really impacted because of what I do at Crossroads? All I do is put out fires, and firefighting seems to be the modus operandi.*

Matt sat up quickly on the couch—he'd fallen asleep and it was now 2 a.m. He turned on the light on the end table. *Maybe the two books Vernon recommended will give me some insight into—and a way out of—this.* Many of the pages he had read so far were underlined and dogeared.

At 4 a.m. Matt finally closed the books and went to bed. In the morning, he felt it was probably best to let Carmen sleep as he left for Starbucks.

"Hey, there you are," Vernon said with a smile, holding his morning coffee in one hand and extending his hand to greet Matt. "Looks like you beat me to this fine establishment today."

Matt wearily stood and shook Vernon's hand. "I wanted to catch up on a little work before you worked on me."

"You *do* look a little worked over." Vernon paused to let Matt explain, but the younger pastor didn't respond. "I hope it doesn't feel like I'm working on you, Matt."

"I'm OK. Really."

Vernon put his coffee on the table, sat down, and continued, "I do know what it's like when it seems that God is working on you. It's not a pleasant experience. Have you been thinking more about our last conversation?"

"I have. In fact, a couple of mornings I've woken up at 2 in the morning and can't get back to sleep because my mind is just racing with things we talked about. In fact, I ordered that book on brokenness you recommended."

"Oh, good. I like a man of action. So where shall we begin today?"

"Well, I guess I'm pretty curious to find out more of what needs to happen inside of me if I'm going to ever help our congregation become this sort of dream church you mentioned yours had become for you."

"Yes, pain is the mother of most change. Only when we're so frustrated with the status quo will we be willing to give up the security of the familiar, even when the familiar is in itself less than we desire. Before the Promised Land comes the wilderness."

"That feels like what I've been in the last few years: wilderness. I guess right now I'm more open to something new than any time in my life.

"With all this build up, I'm getting a little nervous." The two men chuckled.

"Well, I need to ask these questions up front because, although pain is the mother of change that endures, there's always a price for change. In other words, Matt, for you to obtain the kind of dream church that you want, you'll have to be willing to pay the price for that to happen. A lot of pastors are not willing to do that."

"Well, what does it cost? I'm not going to buy something without knowing how much it costs."

"That's what I'd like to talk about today: What it's going to cost you to adopt this new idea that I have in mind for you. I'd guess that most pastors are unwilling to do what it takes to cause change in their churches."

"Why? Why would pastors not be willing to pay the price? After all, they willingly took on a job that pays hardly anything, opens them up to constant critique, and forces them to be on call 24/7—not to mention dealing with the dark side of human nature."

Vernon chuckled. "Why don't we? That's a very good question. I think most of us struggle with paying the price because what I'm going to suggest to you is counterintuitive for most of us as pastors. It's unlike what we've been taught and how we've seen the ministry modeled. What I'm trying to say is, it's not easy to let go of old habits or years—perhaps even centuries—of tradition. But that's the price you'll have to pay, if you want to go down this road."

"OK…" Matt said, as his cell phone interrupted him. "Yeah, hi…I'm sorry, too. I know it's been hard…I love you, too." He hung up his phone and explained, "I need to pick up a gallon of milk on the way home. And some flowers and dark chocolate. It's a long story, but I think it's going to end well."

Matt paused and took a long sip from his coffee cup. "Your challenge is enough to drive a man to drink. I don't know the price, so I can't say I'm willing to pay it, but I do believe I want to know what this price is you're talking about. There's got to be a better way of growing people."

"Oh, it's worth it," Vernon said. "There's no doubt in my mind that if I'd started out of seminary with this kind of training and thinking, my life would have been far better a lot sooner. My first two church experiences were a lot like yours. There's got to be a reason that the average pastoral tenure is three and a half years per church. That's just long enough to realize that there must be greener grass somewhere else."

"You've been talking to my wife, haven't you?"

"That's the problem; there is no quick fix or easy solution. And just repeating what you're doing now, somewhere else, isn't the solution either."

"That's OK. If I hear another seminar on *How to Grow Your Church in 10 Simple Steps* or read another book with ABC solutions, I'm going to heave my coffee grande. One thing ministry has taught me is that there are no easy answers when it comes to growing people."

"How true, my friend, but there are solutions. Most pastors are cutting down the forest with an ax, when there's a chainsaw at their disposal. I began my ministry in a rural area, right when a brand-new type of hay baler was invented. It used to be that when farmers cut and baled hay, the bales were 40 to 50 pounds and had to be picked up off the ground by a couple of people, stacked on a flatbed trailer, and then re-stacked into a barn or haystack. This took a lot of time and was pretty labor intensive.

"Then someone invented a new machine that allowed one farmer to roll hay into a huge bale weighing hundreds of pounds and move it with a tractor attachment—by himself. Productivity shot way up. But there were a lot of farmers who, in spite of the obvious difference, weren't willing to give up on the old machinery."

"So you're asking me if I want a new hay baler?"

"You're quick. That's exactly what I'm asking," Vernon said with a chuckle.

"So what can be so different about what it is you do, than what I'm doing, or what any other typical pastor in the country is doing? No disrespect, mind you."

"None taken. The answer to your question isn't a 'what' but a 'how' and a 'who.' Most conferences and books try to sell you on the what, but this is quite different. Let me cut to the chase. Here's the price you're going to have to pay. If you're going to ever see your dream church, you're going to have to give up the traditional model of pastoring. You know, where the pastor is the central source of ministry. And you're going to need to begin seeing yourself as an equipper of other ministry leaders, who will in turn equip their ministry team members. To implement that in your weekly ministry will require a significant self-image switch, not to mention a practice and ministry structure that looks quite different from the typical church."

Matt sat silently, trying to process what Vernon had just said. "Run that by me again."

"The price you'll have to pay, to see the kind of ministry you want and to experience the joy you seek, will require you to give up on the traditional role of the pastor."

"How has it changed you? You still preach on Sundays. You come to Starbucks to work on your message, like me. Westover is bigger and more involved in the community than Crossroads, but I'm thinking, if I can be honest…"

"Please do."

"No disrespect, but I've been thinking that the difference between us is that you've been at your church longer and the church has just grown faster—for whatever reason—and you're able to hire more staff and have more programs that attract people."

"It's true in part that we do many of the same things as any other church, including yours. But how we got to this point—the level of spiritual growth I now see in our people, and the fact that I'm home most nights and enjoying ministry more than ever—is the confirmation to me that the price I paid several years ago was the right one and well worth it."

"I'm all ears. I'd love to learn what you've learned."

Vernon leaned over and pulled out a yellow pad and pen from his folder. "I do e-mail, but I'm still pretty much a pen and paper guy. All right, here's the typical church."

Vernon drew a circle in the middle of the paper and then extended lines out from the main circle, with smaller ones at the ends of the lines.

"Sometimes I think best by drawing things. So this middle circle is the pastor. In most churches, the pastor is the center of ministry activity. He or she preaches, calls on the sick, runs board meetings, is part-time janitor; and dabbles in any

number of other things such as
age-group ministries, small groups,
fundraising, counseling, Sunday
school, evangelism, discipleship;
not to mention weddings, funerals,
and community roles. Although
no pastor does it all alone, the best
ministry, the certified ministry,
comes from the pastor. Everyone
else tends to be in more of a
support role for the pastor who's
been ordained and qualified as the
primary ministry performer.

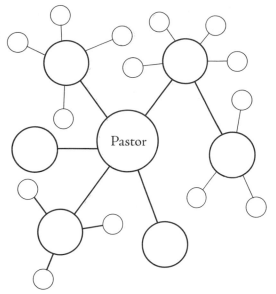

"The problem with this,"
Vernon continued, "is that there's
just one pastor. About 90 percent of the churches in America are under 200 in average
attendance. Is it really possible for one person to directly respond to the needs of that
many people?"

"I see what you're saying, but what's the difference between one person doing
most of the ministry and a larger church like yours that hires more people to serve
more people?"

"Exactly! That's my point."

"What do you mean?"

"Most churches, even the big ones, tend to buy into the pastor-driven ministry
model, where you hire talented staff as the doers of all that is considered 'qualified
ministry' in a church. If there's one thing that the church growth movement has
taught us, it's that you can attract large crowds and not see transformed lives
as a result. The church health movement taught us that if you work on your
weaknesses, you'll be healthy. But neither of those things is enough...here's what
I mean."

Vernon took another sheet of paper and drew a big circle, then a smaller one on
the inside wall of the large one. Then he began drawing some smaller circles within
the circle and a few lines going to the first smaller circle, and then several smaller
circles filling the page that had lines connecting them with each other.

"If the big circle represents the local church, a microcosm of the body of Christ, then this first circle off to the side represents the pastor." Vernon pointed to the circles as he referred to them. "The pastor is directly connected to a few of the other circles that are leaders, people with influence gifts. The pastor disciples and develops these individuals, who are then unleashed to organize the rest of the congregation members and their gifts. The pastor is not the center of ministry, but rather a catalyst to unleash others to serve one another."

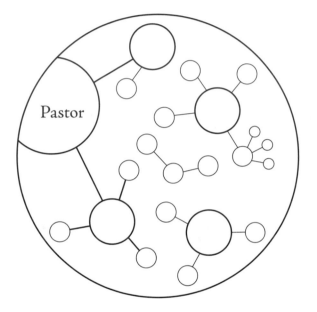

It's Not Your Church

"**S**o what's the price of doing ministry this way?" Matt asked.

"You tell me," Vernon responded. "What do you think it would cost a typical pastor to change from the first graphic to the second?"

"Well, I suppose that might depend on how the pastor is wired and what the congregation expects of him, but in some cases, it might be kind of expensive."

"And why is that?"

"Because that's not how most of us were taught. You'd be leaving a lot of tradition if you really did that. Bucking the way things are."

"And," Vernon added, "it would also affect the way we think about ourselves. We'd have to check our egos at the door, not be seen as the local experts, have to share the limelight, you know."

"Hmm, I hadn't thought about that."

"I don't think most pastors go into the ministry for ego-stroking, but whether we admit it or not, there is a certain amount of esteem that comes from being the center of attention and the representative of God among a group of people."

"Ah, the sage on the stage. One of my professors used to like that phrase."

"Matt, there's a seductive element of being the person with all the answers, the knower of all things important regarding God and eternal matters. That makes it pretty difficult to admit we're wrong or to say we don't know something. As a result, we begin pretending we're more put together than we really are. What other price might there be to pay?"

"I suppose if you're not the center of ministry at a church, then there would be some church attendees upset with you because they expect the pastor to be there for them. I mean, if you don't call certain people when they're sick, or visit them in the hospital, you hear about it big time."

Vernon smiled.

"That's true, in spite of how many of their friends already visited them. 'Oh, but Pastor didn't come visit me, the dirty dog.' Give me the tights and cape. I'll come flying into your room, the big S on my chest: Superpastor. More powerful than a locomotive; able to leap tall buildings with a single bound."

"Oh brother, have we got a few of those people."

"But in the corner of our minds, we kind of enjoy that, don't we?" Vernon asked, nudging Matt's elbow with his.

"Sometimes it *does* feel good."

"Sure it does. It's normal. We're human. But it's not good for the church and maybe not for our souls."

"So what do you do, ignore people when they need a call?"

"No, not at all. Delegating ministry is not abdicating responsibility but rather preparing others to use their gifts. In Acts 6, the apostles were hearing complaints from the widows who weren't being cared for, but did they give up what they were doing to run over and feed them? No. But did they say, 'Hey, take care of it yourself'? No. They found people with the right gifts and empowered them so that they could do what they were gifted at doing."

"That's true, but it seems that you're still going to make some people upset."

"Welcome to leadership, Matt. What do you think Jesus did in Mark chapter 1, after he'd gotten up early in the morning to pray? He came down to find the disciples fretting about not knowing where he was, because people had lined up early to meet him. Jesus said, 'Oh really? Well, let's go to another city.' Probably ticked them off; certainly disappointed them. But he had to be about his Father's business because he'd paid the price to hear God, which in turn required him to sacrifice pleasing folks."

Vernon took a sip of his coffee and continued, "The problem with a lot of us in the ministry is that we love people so much we're unwilling to disappoint them. We're people pleasers. When we can't please them, we feel bad. So we either let our disappointment with ourselves eat at us, which makes us grouchy with our families and everybody else, or we give into it and run ourselves ragged, trying to make everyone happy. That's a price to pay."

"The way you're describing it sounds like there's a need for some intervention."

"That's right, the interaction between pastor and church often does reflect the codependent relationship we see in families where there are addictions. Have you ever been in a recovery group?"

Matt shook his head as Vernon spoke, "I sought some professional counseling a few years ago. Part of that counseling was being involved in a 12-step group. You want to check your ego at the door? Participate in one of those groups. It's one thing to preach on humility, but quite another to experience it in a group like that. I think it would do good for someone to intervene in congregations where the pastor is overworked and stressed out, trying to please everyone, and the congregation is still whining and complaining that the pastor's not doing more."

Matt nodded thoughtfully.

But Wait, There's More

"What else might it cost?" Vernon continued.

"That's not enough?" Matt asked, laughing. He sat back and stared at the ceiling grid, as if searching for another answer. "Well, I suppose some pastors would feel like they're giving up on the way things are to be done, you know, tradition and theology."

"Bingo! Admitting that maybe—just maybe—we've adopted a ministry model that is not as clearly defined in Scripture as we've been taught can be pretty disconcerting. I can tell you that I was never told to pastor the way I do now. The only models I'd seen were the pastor-centric ones."

"But that seems so...so dangerous. I mean, isn't that our calling and our professional training? It feels so risky to put ministry into the hands of the people. They're all over the place spiritually, and some of them theologically, not to mention their busyness, so I shudder to think of what the church might be if we started turning them loose."

"Well, I'd say that's your job...to make sure that Scripture and good doctrine are taught. But the question is: Do you have to be the only one doing it? And how doctrinally pure do you need to be to give a cup of water to someone who is thirsty, or to care for a child, or to organize a group of people to build a house for the poor, or to facilitate a meal for someone who's just lost a loved one?"

"I see what you're saying, but it just doesn't seem to happen that way."

"It does in our church, but I had to pay a price, Matt. Every pastor does. It means giving up control. It's not your church."

"I know that. But that's what makes me feel so responsible, because God is holding me responsible for it. I take my job very seriously."

"Of course you do. I never doubted that. I know you're a committed minister. But it's his church and that means that most of us pastors need to let go of it and let the people with God-given gifts use them in significant ways. You see, it's all about us, but it's not really about us."

"I don't get it."

"I mean that for a church to reach its God-given potential, it's got to begin with pastors who embrace a new way of doing things. A way that moves pastors out of the center of qualified ministry and moves them into a role of preparing others to serve each other—so that other people can reap the benefits of seeing their lives impact others."

Vernon paused for effect, then continued.

"That's the paradox, but then the Bible is full of them, isn't it? Jesus said if you want to gain your life, lose it; for a seed to grow, it must die; if you want to be first, be last; if you want to lead, serve. The role of the pastor in the local church is to act like a fuse that ignites the church to reach its potential. You are the catalyst, not the center of ministry."

Matt leaned back in his chair, locked his hands behind his head, and looked up at the ceiling. He could feel the tears just under the surface—had he really been doing it so wrong all these years? He tried to control his voice as he spoke, "I think I know what you mean, but I'm not sure."

Vernon nodded, then said, "I mean that for you to lead your church into the Promised Land God has for it, you're going to have to leave your homeland as a traditional pastor. Those of us who've been raised by the institutions of the church have been taught to believe that it's primarily about us, which ironically has kept us from accomplishing our goals. In some ways, we've become our own worst enemy, because we've bottlenecked the potential of our church by trying to get all things vital to the church to flow through us. The sad thing is that in most churches, the people let us. They let us get in their way. If I had it to do over, I'd have started from the get-go, but I never knew. No one told me, or taught me, or modeled for me."

"You're talking about letting go of a lot of what I've been trained to do."

"Trained or taught?"

"Well, I guess taught or modeled. I guess most of us really don't get a lot of skill development in our formal education."

"Nor do we discover what it is we're really good at. We're taught that our roles are to preach, but let's be honest: A lot of pastors just aren't strong communicators. They may be really great at administration, or they love discipleship, or evangelism, or pastoral care. Others are great preachers, but not so good at the administration part. When pastors try to do things outside of their sweet spot, everyone suffers."

"I relate to that. I've been doing a lot of things I'm not crazy about, and as a result, not getting to do what I think I'm good at."

"If the body works right, everyone should be doing what they're best at three-fourths of the time—and that includes the pastor. That's our goal on staff. I know of a church near Chicago that's running more than 5,000 people, but the guy who started it was a businessman with the gift of leading, not preaching. So they use sermons on DVD from a strong teaching church."

Matt's eyes widened. "They do what?"

Vernon laughed. "That pastor is willing to pay the price of not being in the spotlight on Sunday morning. He uses his gifts to cast vision and organize the church effectively. If we let leaders lead, preachers preach, and disciplers disciple, we'd all be better off."

"That's not how churches work today, is it?"

"Not very often."

*I'd Get Fired
for That*

Vernon reached for his ringing cell phone and read the screen. "I'm sorry. This is my private line. Do you mind if I take it?"

"No problem," Matt answered.

"Hello, this is Vernon…OK…Did they tell you what the doctor said?…Uh-huh…That's important. Well, have you contacted Mindy on the care team?…OK, I forgot she was out of town. What about Phil?"

Matt felt badly for Vernon. He was needed by someone in his congregation, but here he was, spending time with a guy from another church. He wanted to interrupt him—to encourage him to respond to the call. They could reschedule any time, but it didn't seem appropriate, so he remained quiet while Vernon continued.

"Cheryl, let's have Phil cover it…Right, but let me know if that doesn't work and I'll brainstorm with you some more. I appreciate you keeping me in the know on this. Thanks. Talk to you later."

"Sorry about that," Vernon said as he folded up his cell phone. "There's a man in our church who's been a part of it for many years; he's now in hospice. He's taken a turn for the worse, and our care team coordinator wasn't sure what to do, since a couple of her team are out of town and unavailable."

"Hey, I understand if you need to leave."

"Oh no, she just wanted to make sure the bases were covered."

"Vernon, really, I don't mind at all if you need to get away. We can reschedule."

"We're good. Really. She wanted to keep me informed, but we have someone else taking care of it."

Matt leaned back. "Man, if that were me—and people found out that I was having coffee, in town, with another guy—I'd get fired."

Vernon smiled. "Well, we're not just drinking coffee and shooting the breeze. We're talking kingdom business here."

"I know, I know, it's just what it might appear to others."

"You've got to realize, Matt, that once you get into this, it's a different paradigm. You really do come to understand that other people are better than you at things. When it becomes a part of your culture, people begin to expect it. So that when new people show up, they embrace their ministry."

"It just doesn't make sense to me. I know we live in the same community, but your people sound so different from mine."

"It's how we're created. God works through people in their gifts. When you buy into that, you look at everyday ministry significantly differently."

"**A**ll right, where were we?" Vernon asked. "Oh yes, more costs. The next big price to pay, if you're going to embrace this equipping value, is the critique and criticism of your congregation. Some of them have come to think of their pastor in a certain way, and they need to change how they see you and themselves. People don't always take kindly to people who meddle with their lives. It means they're now going to be accountable to God to use their gifts inside and outside the church. Receiving ministry from other people who aren't the pastor is going to rub some people the wrong way. Are you going to be able to handle the heat?"

Matt sighed. "I can see how that could be a problem."

"For example, I began thinking *Why am I the only one qualified to do hospital calls?* I looked around our congregation and found a man who works at the Ford assembly plant. He's good with people and has the gift of mercy, but no one would confuse him with a pastor."

"What happened?"

"Well, it went better than I thought. I began taking Bill with me on hospital calls. Then he found some others who enjoyed doing that and trained them. I'm just not that good at it, but Bill and his team are."

"How did the people respond?"

"You know, most of them responded really well. One woman was offended that the pastor never called on her in the hospital, and she ended up leaving the church because of it. You'll have to be ready for some of that, but I was really surprised how few people said anything. In fact, I have to admit that it bothered me a bit when people would come up after church and say, 'Oh Bill came and prayed for me when I was getting ready for surgery' or 'Sarah sat with our whole family when Dad was in the hospital; it meant so much to us.' I kinda thought *They don't need me anymore.* But then I realized that their needs were being met by God through others. Bill and his team were able to use their gifts in a meaningful way, and I was freed to focus on things that I'm more gifted at doing."

"You only lost one person? That's amazing considering the size of your congregation!"

"Oh my, no. I mean we lost one family directly related to the issue of hospital calls. We've lost dozens when we started to take this value seriously, in part because many people aren't used to a pastor who doesn't bend over backward to meet all their needs; and they resist taking responsibility for spiritual growth that comes by using their own gifts. Who knows how many others have never become members of Westover, once they discovered what kind of church we are. That's OK. Ultimately the payoff is much greater, but you're going to lose people over any significant church change issue. That's why you want to make sure you pick the right one."

Vernon stirred his coffee and continued. "What I learned through the hospital calling example is that we as pastors often put undue pressure on ourselves to perform a certain way, even beyond what our congregation members expect. People just want to know there is someone who cares, and if that person is more gifted then I am, they end up appreciating it more than if I try to muddle in areas I'm not good at. I guess it became more of an ego issue for me at first than anyone else."

"That's interesting because I do feel that inner pressure."

"People come to expect certain things from their pastor, Matt, but sometimes we're to blame for that. You'll be messing with their assumptions a bit. Your job will be to help re-educate them in terms of Scripture and realistic expectations."

"So is there a prize at the end of these prices? I'm starting to wonder."

"Oh yes! This approach to ministry is most amazing, but it's going to get worse before it gets better. For a while, you're going to be straddling between two ministry paradigms, trying to keep up what is going while also working on the new thing. For a while you'll have more meetings and find yourself working harder. But that's OK because this process is a marathon, not a sprint."

The two men talked more. The longer they talked, the more Matt resolved not to go back to the way he'd been accustomed to pastoring, even though he wasn't quite sure what the new change would require at this point. He felt broken and yet also very hopeful that perhaps the church of his dreams did exist: where people were committed, growing, and impacting their community. He had no desire to do business as usual.

principle

Pastors desiring their church to reach its potential must be willing to pay the price of changing their own pastoral self-image and their approach to ministry.

.

the
PARADIGM

the shift

prepare: equip, develop, and train

WDJD

tyranny of the urgent

WDMD

WDPD

what's next

doing dishes

THE PARADIGM

The Shift

"Come on," Vernon said, standing and taking a long swig from his cup. "Let's get in the car. I have something to show you."

Matt quickly put his notebook into his computer bag and zipped it.

"Where are we going?"

"You'll see."

The two men got into Vernon's car and headed west. Matt wondered where Vernon was taking him. He certainly felt comfortable with his newly found mentor, but the discovery process was still very interesting. He wasn't sure what to expect. After several minutes, Vernon pulled into a parking lot of a commercial building with the name of a large, West Coast seminary on it. Matt and Vernon walked into the extension campus library.

Vernon waved to the man behind the checkout counter and weaved his way through the book stacks to a table area at the back of several rows of stacks.

"Have a seat," Vernon said, motioning to a chair beside the table. "I thought it might help to explain this next principle in a theological library. You know, to add more clout to my argument. You can almost smell church history in these stacks, can't you?" He tilted his head back and sniffed dramatically.

"Matt, we've been taught to believe that our call as pastors is to be the primary ministry doers in our churches. But when we do this, over the long haul, we end up hindering people's growth, not to mention the quality of ministry they receive because of our limited capacities. I think the worst part is that we're selling ourselves short. You know what your problem is?"

"No."

"Pastor Robinson," Vernon said, lightly poking his index finger into Matt's shoulder, "you've been setting your ministry goals much too low."

"Wait a second," Matt said, pushing back from the table, nearly knocking over one of the stacks of books. "Oops, sorry. Got a little excited there. OK, what could be more important for a pastor than to provide ministry for his people? That's what we're called to do."

"Is it?" Vernon seemed unruffled by Matt's response.

"Well, sure it is. Everyone knows that pastors are to serve the people as best they can, and in doing so, model what Jesus did."

"Yes, Jesus was a wonderful model for pastors, and no, most pastors don't do what he did. Here's the problem. By being the primary—or the sole—ministry provider, we undercut the service of others. We're adding ministry when we need to be multiplying it."

Matt paused, thinking it over. "Run that by me again."

"Most pastors think that when they go to seminary or through some sort of formal, ministerial program, they're preparing to provide quality ministry to their people. But in reality, their goal should be to become the local seminary for their church."

"Hmm, I've never thought of it that way."

"The objective of the seminary is not to provide ministry but to train ministers."

"Yeah, I guess that makes sense."

"Look at all these books." Vernon pointed to various stacks of commentaries on Exodus, Matthew, Mark, John, 1 Corinthians, Romans, Ephesians, and 1 Peter. "You show me one place in all these books that gives us the biblical grounds for doing what the typical pastor does in any workweek." He paused for effect and then continued, "It's just not there."

Matt looked at the volumes of books in front of him.

Vernon reached for a Bible. "I'm not trying to talk down to you, really, but take a look at Ephesians 4 very closely. I know you've preached from this passage." The familiar sound of thin pages being flipped filled the quiet of the library. "Here it is. OK, Paul says, 'Live a life worthy of the calling you have received. Be completely humble and gentle; be patient, bearing with one another in love. Make every effort to keep the unity of the Spirit through the bond of peace. There is one body and one Spirit—just as you were called to one hope when you were called—one Lord, one faith, one baptism; one God and Father of all, who is over all and through all and in all.'"

Vernon continued, "So the context here is oneness, not division, meaning we're all on the same team. It's not the clergy versus the laity, the called versus the uncalled, the enlightened versus the ignorant. So we have to start with what we all have in common, God's call in our lives. But how this common call is played out is quite different, depending on how God has gifted us.

"In verse 7 Paul writes, 'But to each one of us grace has been given as Christ apportioned it.' Verse 11, 'It was he who gave some to be apostles, some to be prophets, some to be evangelists, and some to be pastors and teachers, to prepare God's people for works of service.'

"That's it," Vernon said, as loudly as he dared in a library. "That's our job as pastors and teachers, not to do works of service for people, but rather to prepare, to train, to empower God's people for works of service. But for what outcome? Here it is: 'so that the body of Christ may be built up until we all reach unity in the faith and in the knowledge of the Son of God and become mature, attaining to the whole measure of the fullness of Christ. Then we will no longer be infants, tossed back and forth by the waves, and blown here and there by every wind of teaching and by the cunning and craftiness of men in their deceitful scheming.'

"Isn't it funny, Matt? We're killing ourselves to be all things for our people and serve them to the best of our ability, when that's not our job. Our job is to unleash them, and when that happens—and I think *only* when that happens—then they'll become mature. If I'm always doing my kid's homework, cleaning his room, doing his laundry, and speaking for him, he'll never grow up. So why do pastors think that they can do that with their members? Why do pastors think that merely preaching to people, sitting in a pew week after week, is going to make them strong?

"OK, one more thing—sorry man, you asked me," Vernon said, laughing.

Matt smiled. "Never stop a preacher when he's on a roll."

"OK, feel free to 'amen, brother' any time you like. Look at verse 15. 'Instead, speaking the truth in love, we will in all things grow up into him who is the Head, that is, Christ. From him the whole body, joined and held together by every supporting ligament, grows and builds itself up in love, as each part does its work.'

"The pastor is not the head, Christ is. Speaking the truth in love, in my opinion, is perhaps the greatest single sign of maturity. Tell me, how many people can do this, even though they've been raised in the church all their lives? We both know that if we spoke the truth in love to most of our people, they'd leave. Or worse, they'd stay and try to get *us* to leave."

Matt chuckled. "How true."

"You see, we've got all these body parts sort of just doing their own thing; but we lack the ligaments that hold us together, and therefore aren't growing up in love because everyone's not doing their part."

"Amen, brother," Matt said, smiling as he leaned back in his chair.

"That's our job description in a nutshell," Vernon continued, "to prepare and equip people for works of service. It doesn't just happen by preaching to them. Our job is to ordain them to discover, develop, and deploy their gifts, in the context of a friendship with Jesus. Faith and doing faith are not subjects to be learned, but a relationship to be nurtured. Then and *only* then will people become spiritually mature. Tell me, how many pastors have been trained to do that?"

"Not very many."

THE PARADIGM

Prepare: Equip, Develop, and Train

Matt continued, "I keep hearing words such as *equip*, *develop*, and *train*, but I'm not sure if they're all the same or different. How do you use these terms?"

"Sure, good question," Vernon said. "Well, this is the context we use them in at Westover. I don't think there's necessarily a right or wrong way. To me, equipping is the spiritual process of helping people discover their divine purpose and strengths. The Bible refers to them as 'graces' because they're undeserved and God-given. When I got started, I thought that all I needed to do was preach a message or series once a year, have everyone take a spiritual gifts inventory, and I'd done my job. I was wrong, mostly because I was doing it alone.

"So," Vernon continued, "equipping involves helping people discover their purpose and gifts and then find a place of service inside the church or outside in the community. Development, it seems, is a part of equipping. But it tends to focus more on how a person takes their strengths and raises them to the next level. I guess I'd define *training* as a specific method of development. It teaches a skill that will help the person implement his or her gift more effectively. I think it's more about passing on knowledge that is necessary for changed behavior. Training focuses on skill development, so it usually involves some sort of behavioral response that can be mimicked, monitored, and measured."

"Ah, another alliteration," Matt said, writing down the three Ms.

Vernon chuckled. "A lot of people think they're training when really they're trying to teach. Training involves practical application, *doing*, and feedback. Again, most churches defer to the Western classroom model, and then they think they're training when they're really just passing on information."

"That helps—having a definition of those terms."

"Here, look at it this way, Matt." Vernon opened up his leather paper pad and drew a stick man. "Equipping is about the heart, engaging people spiritually to accept the call of God in their lives. We pastors hold dearly to the concept of 'calling,' because we base our ministry on it. But the Latin word for *calling* can also be translated 'voice' or *vocis*. That's the root of the word *vocation*. That tends to be the laity's term for what God has purposed them to do in life.

"Development has more to do with how we improve ourselves through knowledge, experience, and learning from others. It's more of a head matter." Vernon pointed to the stick figure's head. "Now, training has more to do with how our gifts get out of us. It's skill-oriented, so we use the symbol of a person's hands to represent these." He wrote the word "training" and drew a line to the stick figure's hands.

"Can you give me an example of that?"

"Sure. Let me think." Vernon paused. "OK, I'm working with a couple of young leaders who will make great board members down the road. We're in a Bible study that has to do with purpose. In the study, we're talking about how God has gifted them. That's equipping them, helping them discover God's blueprint for their lives.

—— **Development**

—— **Training**

Equipping

"Then, together we'll go over some Peter Drucker materials on how nonprofits function. This is development—taking their gifts of management and leadership and giving these guys a sense of how they can use this in the church realm, which can be quite different than the corporate realm.

"After that, they'll be invited to apprentice, which includes sitting in and observing board meetings, without any voting power, and being assigned a seasoned member who'll mentor them. That's the training aspect."

"That's amazing. I can't believe you do all that."

"Well, all our ministries aren't that clear or developed, but when it comes to leadership, I don't want to rely on chance or trial and error. There's too much at stake."

Matt continued, "So if the pastor's role is to prepare others for ministry, why have we missed the boat so far?"

Vernon laughed. "I have no idea. To the best of my knowledge, sometime after the early church got going, we began to see the formal development of the pastoral function in the church. After Constantine made it OK to be a Christian—and the clerical training system began to emerge—the local priest or pastor seemed to pull away from the common Christian. Granted, there had been prophets and priests throughout the Old Testament, but the New Testament gave a new spirit to this role. We didn't need a priest; we had a High Priest, Jesus. Ephesians chapter 4 gives pastors their job description but without much detail. The modern pastoral model almost seems to be a product of economy, in that the typical church could only afford one staff member to oversee both the teaching and church management, so people began to expect more and more to be done by the local 'paid professional.'"

Matt nodded. "That makes sense. But it still doesn't explain how so many people could be wrong for so long."

"Why do we think we're any smarter than anyone else who's deviated from God's best? Differentiating tradition from original meaning is difficult. We begin assuming that our predecessors are right, without investigating why."

"OK, give me a biblical example of a different way of pastoring."

"Well, let's start with our Founder, Jesus," Vernon said with a smile. "WDJD, What *Did* Jesus Do? I think it's important not only to analyze what Jesus said and taught, which is what we usually do, but also to understand *how* Jesus operated—his methods. If you want to most effectively impact people, what would you do? Jesus, being God, certainly knew the best way to get things done, don't you think?"

"Definitely!"

"All right, then why did Jesus invest a majority of his limited time with just 12 people?"

"Well, I guess he wanted to make sure he left a few leaders who could continue his work."

"Exactly. He put most of his ministry effort into training leaders who'd be able to expand what he began. He focused on leaders."

"So what about the times he taught and fed the multitudes?"

"To be honest, those times seem to be pretty few and far between. I think that a lot of his public ministry was primarily designed to provide places where he could model and then do on-the-job training with his protégés. Sometimes, like at the Sermon on the Mount, he began by teaching the Twelve but crowds gathered to eavesdrop. Jesus' approach to pastoring wasn't to take his ministers away to a secluded spot and dump a lot of info on them, but rather to give them hands-on experiences and then debrief with them afterward."

"So how could a pastor do this? People expect you to serve them, call on them in the hospital, preach, and do all these things."

"Our job is to retrain them, to educate them how Jesus operated. Do you know the only place in the Bible where Jesus is said to be 'full of joy'?"

"Not off the top of my head."

"That's OK, I didn't either. It's in Luke 10, after the 72 returned from doing ministry. I think it's because he realized *they're getting it*. Interesting, isn't it, that his greatest joy came not after he'd done a great ministry deed or taught multitudes, but after he'd unleashed those whom he'd been developing."

"But Jesus wasn't a pastor. He was itinerant, moving around a lot. That's a different model than today's pastor."

"Not necessarily. He simply took his 'church' with him wherever he went." Vernon thumbed through his Bible to chapter 8, then continued. "Here's how Luke describes it: 'Jesus traveled about from one town and village to another, proclaiming the good news of the kingdom of God.'

"But now look at verse 2: 'The Twelve were with him, and also some women who had been cured of evil spirits and diseases: Mary (called Magdalene) from whom seven demons had come out; Joanna the wife of Cuza, the manager of Herod's household; Susanna; and many others.' The 12 named male disciples, Mary, Joanna, Susanna, and 'many others' made up his 'congregation' of 72, according to Luke chapter 10. They traveled with him, gaining new and varied experiences in this training. Geography and space were immaterial. Why would we want to deviate from our leader's methodology?"

"I don't know."

"I don't either. If you analyze Jesus' approach, it is a classic training method. He gathered leaders, students, and then taught them. Then he said, 'watch me' and then 'join me' and then 'go try it yourself.' Afterward he gathered them back and said, 'How'd it go?' 'Couldn't cast out the demons? Oh, no problem. Next time, try fasting and praying.'"

"So why don't we train that way? I mean, if it's so obvious, why don't we teach pastors to do that?"

"I don't think it's a conspiracy or dark sin. I think it's more that we're products of our environments, and over the years, we've just gradually bought into the westernized educational philosophy. We think that if we bring people together, preach at them for a while, and then say 'Go get 'em', people will do it. That doesn't work. What it creates are biblical intellectuals."

"That makes sense, but that sounds pretty harsh."

"Think about it. The average pastor puts in 25 hours a week in message prep. He gets paid just over $40,000 a year, and there are somewhere around 300,000 churches in the U.S. Add all that up, and you'll see that every week American churches invest over $140 million in preaching. That's a major investment, and what's the return on that investment? Church attendance is on the decline. The percentage of people claiming to know Christ is pretty much unchanged the last three or four decades, and the moral fiber of our culture doesn't seem to be improving. I'm not a fatalist, but you can't convince me that's good stewardship. There's got to be a better way."

Matt shook his head, thinking about Vernon's last statement. "Man, that does seem like a waste of time. So what are we supposed to do?"

"We still have worship and preaching services at Westover, but years ago we stopped thinking it was the main thing we did. It's like our storefront ministry, but it's only the tip of the iceberg. In most churches, it *is* the iceberg. If pastors adopted Jesus' style of ministry, we'd do things significantly different."

"Now there's a paradigm shift!"

"Oh, we're just getting started," Vernon laughed.

Matt's cell phone went off. Matt reached for it, then thought *I'll let voice mail catch it.* Vernon watched Matt's struggle. Matt drummed his fingers, looked at his friend, then impulsively picked it up, careful to avoid eye contact with Vernon.

"Thanks. Hi, this is Pastor Matt...Oh, hi, Tammy. How's it going?...OK. I think John is handling that. What?...Do they need to meet now?...Are you sure?" Matt looked at his watch. "Well, OK, I'll be right there...No, no problem."

"You need to run?" Vernon asked.

"Yeah, I'd better. I'm sorry. Something's come up, and I need to run back to the office for a while. I know we were right in the middle of talking about the biblical examples of this new paradigm, but I'm afraid I'm still stuck in the old one."

"No worries, Matt. Let's try to connect next week."

"That would be wonderful. I'm so sorry."

As Matt drove, he felt frustrated with the interruption. No, he wasn't frustrated as much as he felt embarrassed. In the past, he'd sometimes felt a sense of affirmation when people needed him. He'd come over right away to provide counseling—interrupting what he'd planned—in order to fit other people's schedules. But now he was beginning to feel embarrassed for ending his meeting with Vernon so abruptly, appearing to be at the beck and call of his congregation members. Even though Vernon's congregation was significantly larger than his, his friend was able to make time to invest in him; but he couldn't make the time because his church needed him.

By the time Matt arrived at the church office, he was truly irritated by feeling perpetually on-call. His clergy collar seemed to be attached to a long leash, held by all the church attendees. Funny, he didn't even wear a clerical collar, but it felt like one, and a tight one at that. Although he knew it was the assumed "pastoral thing to do," he was starting to learn from Vernon that there was a better way.

"Hey, Tammy," Matt greeted his ministry assistant as he came into the office.

"Sorry to interrupt your meeting, Pastor," Tammy whispered respectfully, "but the Thompsons said they really needed to see you. I assumed that since you'd met with them before, you'd want me to let you know."

Matt knew it wasn't professional, but he rolled his eyes. "No problem, Tammy.

Where are they?" he asked, looking around the office sitting area.

"They're in your office," she said. "I told them you were on your way."

Matt nodded, pausing a moment to change gears internally so he could respond graciously to the Thompsons. Even though he was certain it was not an emergency, Matt felt somewhat obligated to be there for them since their family had been active at Crossroads for several years.

After nearly an hour of talking with the Thompsons, the couple left. Matt leaned back in his chair. *This is what Vernon is trying to teach me, isn't it?* he pondered. *I'm like a puppet on a string and for what? The Thompsons still have their problems, and I interrupted a meeting to come rescue them. At least they know I care. But how much did it matter, really? Have I developed people the way Jesus did? Am I just doing this to feel good about myself, or am I helping people grow and get better?*

Matt picked up the phone and got through to Vernon's voice mail.

"Hey, it's Matt. I want to apologize again for having to cut our meeting short. I realize I need to start doing things differently. It was a bit of a false alarm. I'm sure someone else could have taken the call, or at least we could have handled it in a different way. Anyway, I'm looking forward to our next meeting and learning more about this paradigm shift. I think I'm primed to get a lot out of it." Matt hung up the phone, pursed his lips, and slowly shook his head. *There has to be a better way.*

"Hey, thanks again for rescheduling," Matt said.

"Really, no problem," Vernon responded. "OK, last time we talked about how Jesus approached his pastoral ministry. Now let's look at the Old Testament."

"Sounds good."

The two pastors were meeting again at the seminary library. Vernon pulled a commentary on Exodus from the stacks. "When God was organizing his people, he provided structure, not just rules and regulations." Vernon set the commentary on the table and picked up the Bible, moving his fingers lightly through it. "Check out Exodus 18. You know the story. Moses was burning both ends of the candle, trying to pastor his huge congregation. He's exhausted and the people are frustrated because they're waiting in line all day. Moses had sent his wife and kids to stay with her dad, more than likely because she'd been nagging him about never seeing him. Sound familiar?"

"Ouch," Matt groaned.

"So along comes the father-in-law, Jethro. He's probably gotten an earful, but he's a shrewd dude. He doesn't tell Moses he's a lousy son-in-law. Jethro simply comes alongside him and says, 'What you're doing is not good.'"

"Smart father-in-law. Very smart."

"Exactly. Then God advises Moses through a relative instead of a burning bush this time. Jethro said to find capable people who will oversee groups of 10, 50, 100, and 1,000. Only handle the most difficult cases yourself. Moses reproduced himself, stabilized the nation, developed others, and the result was better congregational care."

"Yes, but Moses wasn't a pastor."

"But he was. He was also a surrogate king, prophet, and military general. He was God's representative. This was God's blueprint for organizing his people. Of course, Scripture never tells us how Moses did it. It simply suggests he took the advice and implemented it."

"Implementing it—that's the common challenge, isn't it? A lot of the time, it seems like we're missing the 'how-to' in the Bible, doesn't it?"

"Very true. Obviously, Moses needed to do some assessing, some interviews, seeing who'd become leaders during the enslavement in Egypt, and checking out references of sorts. No doubt there was some training so that each leader knew his responsibility."

"Sounds like a big, multilevel operation."

"True, so what did Moses do? Like Jesus, he invested his attention on raising leaders who would in turn organize and care for the bulk of the people."

"That makes a lot of sense; but I couldn't do that because I'm consumed with all the other stuff."

"Just like most pastors, Matt. And I can pretty well guarantee it got worse for Moses before it got better. Every transition is like that."

Vernon continued as he moved his finger down the column of his Bible. "OK, now here's the kicker. In Exodus 19:6, God says my people will become a nation of priests. How's that for a self-image transformation? God's informing these recent slaves that they're going to become a nation of priests. As far as I know, our calling has never been changed. It's reiterated again in 1 Peter 2. From the start of the Bible through the end, all of God's people are to be priests, not just the Levites or the various prophets. They provide a unique service in preparing the priests, but they don't take the place of the nation of priests."

"So why has that never become a reality? I've preached these passages before, about people embracing their responsibility and there not being two doors in heaven, one for 'clergy' and one for 'laity.' But in everyday church life, it doesn't seem to stick."

"Good point. Maybe it's because we're approaching it wrong. Martin Luther acknowledged the priesthood of believers in his 95 theses, but we never seemed to grasp how to implement it in the church. The invention of the Gutenberg press fanned the flames by making the Bible available to the masses, sort of like the Internet today, but we have to do more. The time is ripe for another reformation of sorts. These days, laity are often as educated as clergy, sometimes more. With the Boomers' emergence into second-half life issues and subsequent generations' desire for social impact, you can see why this hunger is growing in America."

"So I'd better get on board or get left behind, huh?"

"Definitely. I'm convinced that now more than ever in recent history, churches that fail to tap the latent potential among their congregants will not make it in the future."

"So you're saying this is more than preaching and teaching the use of spiritual gifts. I've been doing that for years."

Vernon leaned back, with a big smile on his face.

"All right, what did Paul do?" Vernon asked rhetorically. "When you talk about spiritual gifts, you have to look at Paul's ministry." He shuffled the thin leaves of his Bible. "Romans 12, 1 Corinthians 12, Ephesians 4—they all talk about every Christian's unique place in the body of Christ. They tell us that our gifts have one source just like we have one source: Christ. And for us to be unified in our faith and community, we've got to acknowledge the diversity of gifts."

Vernon paused. "But there's another paradox: We're many, but we're one; we're diverse, and yet we're alike. Everyone has a blueprint, a unique DNA that directs us to the niche we fill in the body of Christ. Most spiritual-gifts programs are about filling ministry slots. Ours is about finding fulfilling ministry. There's a big difference."

"I don't understand," Matt said, squinting.

"We'll get to that, but before I forget, let's look at Paul's strategy. Paul's ministry wasn't about serving people. It was about raising leaders and discipling those who would in turn develop others."

"OK, I'm seeing a theme here. But Paul is considered by most to be a missionary, not a local church pastor. He traveled all over the place."

"Don't get geography confused with methodology. Who said you're not to be an urban or suburban missionary?"

"Because I'm not. I'm a local church pastor. Pleasant Valley is my congregation… and yours."

"Ah, Matt, but I'm talking mind-set more than mileage. Paul's aim was to raise up capable leaders who would in turn expand the kingdom. Sometimes he'd visit and at other times write. Sometimes he'd encourage, at other times educate, and a few times confront. He didn't consume his life with weekly message prep or doing hospital calls because he knew that long-term success involved investing in key people who would multiply the ministry."

"Instead of *adding* ministry."

"Exactly. It's about getting the math right. You've probably read some of the new books on missional ministry, behaving more strategically than we have in the past, thinking more like a missionary than pastor."

Matt nodded as he pondered Vernon's words. "I've never thought of myself as a missionary."

"A good missionary doesn't try to become the people's leader. He or she finds the indigenous influencers and disciples them, giving them a heart for ministry. It's a paradigm shift. For instance, type in 'equip' in that high-tech little gadget you carry all the time."

"It's a PDA," Matt said, smiling as he tapped with his stylus. "Here it is: 'to provide, furnish, stock, and supply.' Another dictionary uses the word 'prepare,' 'motivational readiness.' Do you want the Greek as well?"

"Sure."

"Here is it. I've got 20 translations including Hebrew and Greek."

Vernon shook his head in amazement.

"Here's the Greek: 'to fully furnish, to help people reach their potential.'"

"I really do need to get one of those things. Here's the point, Matt. Most pastors think they're equipping when they preach one or two sermons a year on spiritual gifts, or have an assessment available for recruiting people to ministry slots. But that's just a variation of the old school. The paradigm shift takes place only when the pastors realize that equipping is a fundamental value, and that their primary purpose is to champion that value in the local church."

"So preaching on spiritual gifts isn't enough?"

"Not at all. Most pastors preach Ephesians 4, but they operate primarily from a pastor-centric model. I'm not picking on you, but I'm trying to keep it real." Vernon opened his notepad, flipped it around sideways, and began drawing five stair steps. He placed a number 1 on the lowest and numbered the others, 2 through 5, bottom to top. "Nearly every church gets stuck on one of five different levels. On level 1, the pastor serves as Emperor, the primary ministry source, with some 10 to 20 percent of people involved in ministry. At level 2, the pastor serves as Engager, where he shares ministry among the committed core. Between 20 to 40 percent of active attendees are involved here. At level 3, the pastor is an Encourager, promoting the idea that people have gifts and should steward them in the church. Approximately 40 to 60 percent are involved at this level, which is about as high as you can go in the traditional pastoral paradigm. At level 4, between 60 to 80 percent of people are involved. The pastor is an Equipper in terms of helping establish a system that makes sure people discover, develop, and deploy their gifts. At level 5, the pastor becomes an Empowerer. Here 80 percent or more of the church is involved in service and much of that overflows into the community, so that the church is truly impacting. This is where the congregation becomes incarnate, living out its faith beyond the walls, so that those outside the church see our good deeds and we bring glory to God."

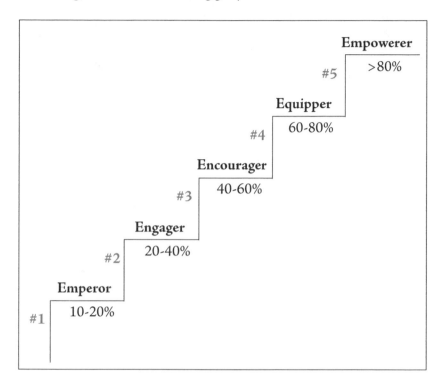

Vernon turned the paper around so it faced Matt and then nudged it toward him.

"Incarnate. What do you mean?" Matt asked, putting his finger on the top step of the diagram.

"I mean that when churches buy into the Western educational model, there's a lot of head knowledge and passive learning, but very little gets implemented. John 1 says that 'the Word became flesh.' Jesus was God incarnate, or as Peterson says in *The Message*, 'The Word became flesh and blood and moved into the neighborhood.'* The goal of discipleship is for God's Word to become incarnate, to be fleshed out in a Christian's life. Without service, people never really live out the Word. We confuse Bible knowledge with maturity."

Vernon took another sheet from his notepad. "Sorry; like I said, I think graphically." He drew an inverted triangle. "The typical church pours on the preaching, teaching, and Bible study, but they do very little in terms of helping people apply it." Then he drew a base-down triangle. "An equipping value acknowledges that Scripture is like good medicine. It's powerful. A little goes a long way. Therefore, we believe in it, but we invest 90 percent of our energy into helping people live it out.

"Another way of looking at it is food," Vernon said, patting his stomach. "I've found that the older I get, the less I need to eat and the more I need to exercise. It's a lot easier to eat than exercise. That's how it is spiritually as well. Spiritual obesity is killing the church."

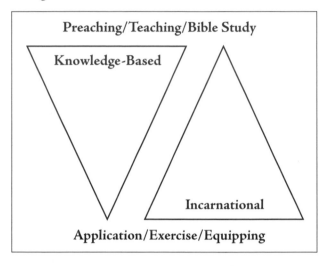

"I really see that. So how does a church get to levels 4 and 5?"

"Ah, thanks for asking; I nearly forgot my point. A church will rarely get beyond 3, never 4, unless there is a paradigm shift in the life of the pastor, staff, and church culture. You see, a leader can't delegate a value, only a task or program."

"I'd think that a church that has people involved inside and outside of the church would have quite an impact on the community."

"Absolutely, Matt. A typical church can only handle about half of its active attendees in service. After that it pretty much hits a saturation point, where people feel unneeded or underutilized. You're always going to have a few ministry openings, no matter how many people are involved. But when you begin to acknowledge people's passion to serve outside the church and unleash them in the community, people really notice."

"So I assume that's helped you grow."

"That's been our most effective outreach. Today, people aren't interested in what you know. They don't want to be converted. But when they see people who call themselves Christians painting a school, building a Habitat home, teaching English to immigrants, and volunteering down at the homeless shelter, they notice. That's the incarnation of Christ, when his body takes on skin. I'm convinced more and more that churches that fail to think externally will have a harder and harder time growing. They'll eventually shrivel up and die."

What's Next

Matt sat at the table, staring back and forth at the two graphics that Vernon had drawn on the sheets of paper.

"So what are you thinking?" Vernon asked. "Does it make sense?"

"It does," Matt said. "It really does. I guess I'm still trying to get my mind around this whole thing."

"Well, you're on a steep learning curve. This stuff has taken me years to figure out, and I guarantee you there was a lot of trial and error. If you think you have to have it figured out before you get started, it's not going to happen."

"It's amazing. When I look at the Scriptures you pointed out, I wonder how the church became what it is today."

"Cultural creep. We've evolved into this role over the years, but it makes sense we're not seeing better results."

"So what does this new paradigm look like? What do I do differently?"

Vernon thought for a moment, looking out the window into the parking lot. "All right, the best way to learn is by experiencing it, but let me give you a few ideas to prime the pump. One simple thing is that you stop using sermon illustrations that feature you as the ministry performer, you know, 'Last week, I was in the hospital visiting Mavis,' or 'John called me to come over and talk to his neighbor about knowing God.' Tell stories about other people affecting others. Share the limelight. Lift them up. Let people tell their ministry stories in person or record a simple videotape. When someone is being baptized, recognize the person who was instrumental in the person coming to know Christ; or if your tradition allows, let that person baptize their friend. If you're really daring, take a few moments at the end of your message for everyone to find a partner and share what they got out of your Sunday message."

"Whoa, that would be radical!"

"Perhaps, but it's our job to do whatever we can to engage people and equip them as priests."

"Makes sense," Matt said, writing notes on his laptop. "That's good."

"Another thing is to analyze your weekly schedule. Literally measure how much time you invest in various activities, and then begin with 10 percent of your time in training others for ministry. Here…" Vernon took his pen and a new sheet of notebook paper. He drew a rectangle and a line from the lower left edge toward the upper right edge of the box.

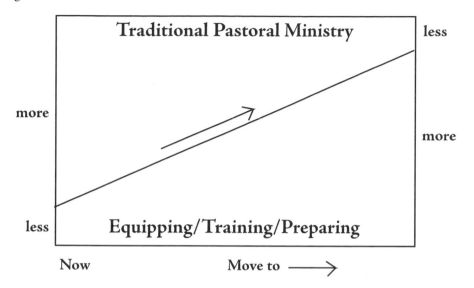

He turned it around and showed Matt. "Right now, most of your time is spent in doing. You're a ministry factory. What we want to do, over time, is begin doing more and more training and preparing, and less and less end-user ministry. You're moving from the assembly-line floor to training and management. Of course, no matter how much of an equipper you become, you'll always do some hands-on ministry in emergency cases and when serving your leadership team."

"Can I have this?" Matt asked, holding up the sheet of paper.

"Sure. Here's another thing. Never do ministry alone."

"What do you mean?"

"I mean as much as you're able, schedule someone else to meet you at the hospital or when you're dropping by someone's home for a visit or even planning a meeting. Use your ongoing to-do list as a training opportunity for developing other ministers. Always have a shadow, someone who is with you, observing how it is you do ministry."

"That sounds like a hassle. It's a lot easier to do it yourself."

"True, it is. But that's part of the price you pay for developing others. Initially, it's more work. It's a pain to work around people's schedules. But over the long haul, you're developing others."

"OK got it," Matt said, tapping on his keyboard.

"And on that note, make sure you have training for whatever you ask someone to do in ministry. The church is about the only place in society where you don't have to have any training to be involved in a role. If you work with the Boy Scouts or Boys and Girls Clubs or schools, chances are you'll go through some rigorous training before you're unleashed. When you do this, two things happen. First, you raise the bar of commitment by saying 'this job is so important, you need to be trained.' Second—"

Matt interrupted, "But people are so busy, they won't take the time to show up for training."

"Raise the bar. Winners aren't interested in wasting their time on things that anyone can do and effectiveness doesn't matter. Besides (and this is the second thing) when you train, you set people up to succeed. When people succeed, they feel good about what they're doing. Most churches guilt people into service, don't train them adequately, and then they wonder why people don't last long. Go figure."

"OK, make sure there's a training component to every ministry," Matt said.

Vernon continued, "And a couple more things you'll do differently as an empowering pastor: In meetings, don't speak first. In fact, let someone else lead the meeting that you've gone over with him or her beforehand. Provide some coaching or find someone who is good at running meetings, but avoid being one of the first ones to speak on an issue. Let everyone participate, and if someone is quiet, seek his or her opinion. Ask more questions than give answers. We pastors are tellers. We're wired to give answers. But as soon as we do, we shut down the development of others and team-building. Use the rule of three: You don't make a comment until at least three others have given their opinions."

"Hmm, that's good," Matt said. He looked at his watch. "I want to honor your time. What's one more?"

Vernon scratched his chin and looked at the tiles in the ceiling. "I'd like to talk about leadership development, but we'll need more time to unpack that one. OK, here's what an empowering pastor does that a traditional one doesn't do. When people call or e-mail or drop by to see you, be very careful about automatically switching into rescuer mode. Set boundaries, not to be aloof or uncaring, but to make sure this is something you should do by yourself, or whether you should use it as a training time or delegate it to others. When people begin to receive ministry from each other, this becomes a part of your church culture. Far too many pastors jump in to rescue because it feels good and they're afraid of what people will think of them if they don't. But if you've been developing others, you'll have those you can call on to serve the needs in your congregation as they arise."

"There is so much to learn. I don't think I'm going to be able to figure this out on my own. I'm going to need your help," Matt said.

"Well, we've come this far. I'm game to unpack this if you are, but we've probably done as much as we can at Starbucks and the library."

"What do you mean?"

"I mean that we should begin watching each other do ministry and we should start involving others in the process."

"What does that look like?"

"I'm not sure. You can come shadow me for a while, watch how I interact with others, and talk to my partner."

"Your partner?"

"Yes, every church that succeeds in becoming an empowering congregation has three things in common. It has a pastor who has made a paradigm shift, a partner who champions the effort, and a process that provides a system for implementing it in the church. Not having even one of these three can hamstring a church from becoming one that reaches its potential. That's what it means to equip."

Matt typed in three words on his laptop: *pastor, partner, process.* "Hey, it's a pastoral alliteration."

"So you know it must be inspired."

"OK, I guess I'm ready to get going."

"Oh, you're already going, Matt. You're just taking it to the next level."

"That's right. I can't believe you're willing to spend so much time on this. You have so much going on."

"Well, when I find a leader who is teachable and motivated, I try to find time to invest. Besides, when you buy into this value, you automatically want to develop and deploy people who are willing. It becomes a part of who you are."

"**Y**ou've got to be kidding!" Carmen exclaimed. "We invested all that money and time in seminary and you find out 10 years later that you've been doing it wrong?"

Matt wasn't sure if his wife was joking or not. "Well, I guess you always keep learning," he said. "I thought you'd be excited to hear what I'm learning."

"Oh hon, I am," she said, flopping next to him on the couch. "It really does make a lot of sense. I just hope this isn't some sort of fad or program or next great secret to church growth. We're getting too old for dream-chasing."

"I know, me too," he said, patting her on the knee.

"Doesn't it make you wonder how so many smart, good people could be doing ministry wrong? What makes Vernon think he's got the right answer?"

"I don't know. In some ways, it's not that we quit being a pastor but it's more about how we minister. I don't have it all figured out, but after he talked to me about biblical models of shepherding, it really got me thinking about why we do what we do. I can't find a lot of scriptural basis for the contemporary pastor's workweek."

"I'm excited for you. I really am. I just don't fully understand it yet. I grew up in a pastor's family and that's not the way Dad did it."

"I know. But do you want us to just repeat what our parents did? You've said yourself how it seemed at times that ministry beat up your parents and didn't seem fair to the kids, even though you respected him."

Carmen rubbed her hands over her face.

"I just wish we knew how it worked better. I've really enjoyed hearing about what Vernon is teaching you. It just seems so different from the way we've done it so far."

"It is. He said it's nothing short of a paradigm shift in terms of how I think about myself and how I function within our congregation. I think we're going to focus more on how it actually looks in our future meetings."

"I'm excited about seeing change. I know God has called us to do more than baby-sit. It just seems too good to be true that you could have more time to do what you're good at, while others are doing what they enjoy and are good at. Speaking of which, how'd you like to help me with the dinner dishes?"

"I don't think clearing the table and doing dishes is in my gift mix."

"Oh yeah, well if you don't come help me I may just leave them here for you while I go to the mall and use my gift of shopping," Carmen said, pulling Matt off the couch.

"All right, you got me," he said, putting his arm around his wife. "Sometimes you just have to do things you're not good at for the sake of the family."

"Amen."

Endnotes

1. Eugene Peterson, *The Message* (NavPress, 2003), 1925

principle

The primary purpose of the pastor is to help people discover, develop, and deploy their God-given gifts for serving others.

the
PARTNER

The Matrix

"**M**att, this is Chris," Vernon said, introducing his "partner" in equipping. Chris was a tall man, a few years younger than Matt, with a big, welcoming grin.

"Hi, Matt," Chris said. "Pastor's told me a lot about you. I've been looking forward to our meeting."

"Thanks," Matt said, shaking hands with Chris.

"Come, let's sit down," Vernon said, motioning the other two men toward a sitting area in his office. "Matt, I wanted you to meet Chris because he's the best I've ever worked with as far as understanding what it is we need to accomplish here at Westover to prepare people for ministry."

"So do you have a clone?" Matt said.

"I'm afraid the closest I can do is a couple of kids," Chris said. "But at 6 and 8, I'm not sure how much help they'd be."

Matt laughed along with Chris and Vernon as they all sat down.

"Vernon, I've had something on my mind since you mentioned you had a partner. If I can be blunt, I remember you said you can't delegate equipping. But that seems like what you've done…"

"I said you can't delegate a value, but if you want this to become a part of your church culture, you have to have a partner or someone who'll champion it—someone who already believes in that value as strongly—or more—than you do. Your partner can help you develop a system for engaging people and assisting ministry leaders to own the value. Here, let me show you." Vernon reached for his pad of paper and turned it sideways. He drew several lines up and down and then at the top wrote the words "youth," "children," "worship," "hospitality," and "admin."

"The typical church has a variety of ministry specialties, like these," Vernon said, pointing to the categories. "The good part is that the ability of these ministries to focus in a specific area is very strategic. Each ministry adds to the entire church by focusing on a certain group of people or type of talent. But the downside is that because of their concentration in one area, they can become ministry islands that tend to operate on their own. The bigger a church gets, the more likely these will be self-functioning and potentially independent from the church as a whole, other than funding and facilities."

"So what does an equipping or lay-mobilization ministry have to do with these?" Matt asked.

"Well, even though most churches never get around to intentionally focusing on empowering others for ministry, those that do often end up creating another ministry department that operates on its own," Vernon said.

"But isn't that a good thing, you know, to actually specialize in this area?" Matt asked.

"It sounds good, but here's the problem," Vernon said. "If you make equipping just another ministry department—like youth ministry, children's ministry, or worship ministry—then it never really takes off. But when a church considers equipping a value—and not just a means for recruiting cheap labor—then the equipping value becomes a part of *all* the other ministry areas. As long as equipping is a program, an appendage of the church instead of a value, it'll never be enough to significantly change the church. It's got to become a horizontal value, not a vertical program. Here…I'll show you what I mean."

Vernon began writing words in the left margin: "equipping," "outreach," and "leadership development," and drew dotted lines from the words across the vertical columns. "These horizontal rows are values in our church. Because equipping is one of our values, it spreads through all the vertical ministry columns.

"Which is why I need my partner—he holds each ministry area accountable to the equipping value. Chris ensures that equipping is practiced in all of the ministry areas. If you don't have someone like Chris, a champion for equipping, then there's a tendency to deviate from that value and your church is not synchronized. You have to make sure that equipping is a part of every ministry in your church—from children's ministry, to youth ministry, to worship, hospitality, and administration."

"That's interesting. So people in the horizontal rows function across ministry areas?" Matt asked, pointing to the left side of the paper.

"Exactly," Vernon said. "For a while, we treated ministry involvement as a separate ministry area, like any of the others. The problem is that it was always seen as sort of a separate entity and the other staff didn't seem to take it seriously. It's kind of like the children's ministry doing their thing, the youth ministry doing their thing, and the worship team doing theirs. We didn't see a lot of interaction going on between our equipping team and the other ministries. Each ministry sort of did its own thing, occasionally asking for help if they couldn't recruit enough workers for an event or program."

	youth	children	worship	hospitality	admin.
equipping					
outreach					
leadership development					

"So do you have people who oversee these other values, such as outreach and leadership development?" Matt asked.

"We do now," Vernon said. "But it's because we're bigger. The reason an empowering ministry needs a key person and team in place is that the sheer logistics and coordination of a lot of people and various ministry leaders requires much more of a concerted effort. It's the most involved value to implement if it's going to be done right."

"So how did you discover there was a better way?" Matt asked.

Vernon laughed. "At first it was trial and error," he said. "We couldn't ever seem to get more than 50 percent of our church involved in ministry service. Plus, we still had staff who didn't seem to buy into the deeper value of equipping. Then we came upon some training that really helped us figure out what we were doing wrong. Three or four of us went to hear Sue Mallory speak at an event. She convinced us that we'd not taken our equipping efforts far enough."

"A church that thinks of equipping as a way to fill ministry slots will rarely ever have more than half of the church involved, and that's pushing it," Chris said. "It's like a parking lot. Once the stalls are full, people just drive on. You either lose people or you create spectators, neither of which helps them grow."

"So were you on staff then?" Matt asked.

"Not at the start," Chris said, "but even when I came aboard, I wasn't paid, if that's what you mean."

"We like our staff to earn their positions first, if possible," Vernon said.

"He means we're cheap," Chris said laughing. The other two chuckled as well.

"Sounds like our budget," Matt said. "So you don't need to start with a paid person."

"Not at all," Vernon said. "Obviously, as your church grows, you'll want to add this paid role quickly, because it's so strategic for the entire church."

"I'm so glad to hear that you have a point person for this role," Matt said. "I was afraid that I'd have to do this by myself, and it just seemed overwhelming."

"That's the point: You can't and shouldn't do it yourself," Vernon said. "Moses had those who supervised a thousand each, implying he had an executive team."

"When would you hire this person?" Matt asked. "I mean, in what sequence? What size should you be, before you prioritize this role?"

"Well, if you asked me, I'd have tried to fill this role from the start," Vernon responded. "Obviously, a pastor has to look at the whole team, meaning the congregation, and figure out what sort of talent is there. But to be honest, if I were planting a church, I'd make the director of equipping, or whatever you title it, the first position to fill."

"What?" Matt asked. "What about a youth pastor or worship leader or even a church secretary?"

"I know, it's not traditional thinking," Vernon said. "We're trained to think talent. But if you want to tap the abilities in your church and elevate ownership—all very key for a new or established church—I'd make sure there was either a paid or unpaid person in this key role of overseeing the equipping process. It's too strategic to wait until sometime down the road when you think you can afford it."

"This isn't a luxury staff position," Chris said, "something only bigger or wealthier churches afford. If you buy the value, you realize how important it is to find a partner who'll help you develop the ministry talent that God has endowed every church with. But it's a lot like mining. You don't always see it on the surface, so you have to dig down a bit to uncover it. Most churches are filled with gold, all the while complaining that they just can't seem to get more people involved."

"When pastors think equipping or ministry involvement is just one more program they have to run, it'll never get off the ground because they're already juggling all these ministry balls," Vernon explained. "Besides, it would be sort of hypocritical if the pastor had to be the person who did all the equipping, organizing, and leading." They all smiled. "This is about team; utilizing multiple people in roles that fit their gifts."

"So how did you figure it out, Vernon? You know, how to get it done," Matt asked.

"Chris will tell you that I didn't figure it out," Vernon said. "Did I, Chris?"

Chris laughed. "Oh, you've done a great job helping me dig for the right answers. Actually at the beginning, I thought he was just being a great coach. I'd come to him with a problem, and he'd ask some key questions such as 'What do you think it will take to get us going?' and 'If you could pick a team to help you, who'd be on it?' I always thought his questions were designed to develop me."

"Actually, they were, because I didn't have a clue," Vernon said.

"That's funny," Matt said.

"You don't have to have it all figured out," Vernon said. "That's the problem. We pastors think we have to have all the answers. If you get the right person in the right place, and give him or her some coaching and support, it's amazing what will happen."

"So what kind of qualities should I look for in this equipping partner?" Matt asked.

"Obviously, you want to find someone who *loves God*, the *church*, and who *you can trust*," Vernon said. "Those are a given for any staff person. But in addition to those, I think there are three specific qualities. One quality of a great equipper is *discernment*. This person needs to have a sense of where a person fits on a team, who the potential leaders are, and why a ministry team may not be functioning well."

"That's interesting. I can't think of a job description I've read that calls for discernment," Matt said, writing notes on his laptop.

"Well, whoever you find to direct your equipping ministry, or whatever you end up calling it, needs to have discernment. They need to be able to read people," Vernon said. "That person also needs the *gift or skill of training*. Your partner is primarily a developer of other trainers, so the ability to come alongside someone, provide instructions, and motivate people to work together is very important."

"You're constantly in some kind of training situation," Chris said.

"What kinds of things do you train?" Matt asked.

"Oh, any number of things," Chris said. "Initially, there are spiritual gifts workshops, followed up by one-on-one interviews. Then every ministry is required to have a training component for new people, as well as periodic continuing education for those already on the team."

"How do you ever find the time to do all this?" Matt asked. "I mean, we feel lucky if we get people to come five minutes before they're to teach a Sunday school class or serve on a hospitality team."

"We've discovered that when you invest in people, they realize how serious you are about the results and how important the mission is," Chris said.

"Plus, you improve their chances of succeeding, which of course makes them feel more effective and appreciated," Vernon said. "The director of equipping is constantly training and helping others create effective training."

"We can let you see some of our training resources," Chris said. "We call it Westover U."

"That would be great," Matt said.

"The third quality you'll want in a partner is the *ability to organize*," Vernon said. "When you're in this role, there are a lot of details to handle because you don't want people to feel like they're falling through the cracks. They need to feel appreciated. This takes a *systems thinker*, someone who can organize both people and structures. By systems thinker, I'm not implying someone who loves flowcharts more than people. Obviously, this person needs to enjoy people because equipping involves a lot of interpersonal interactions."

"But you're saying this is not the typical *star* candidate," Matt said.

Vernon chuckled. "No, it tends to be counterintuitive, and I'm afraid they don't emphasize these kinds of skills in seminary or ministerial preparation. So you either need to grow them yourself or find someone who has been doing something similar, like working with a nonprofit organization or in the area of corporate human resources. Hopefully the supply of trained, qualified people will change as more and more churches develop these types of people."

"We're actually working with a few progressive seminaries and Bible colleges to embrace a certification program for equippers," Chris said. "There's now an informal network of higher-ed professors who work with us in forming these courses."

"Sounds interesting," Matt said. "So what do you do after you find someone with these basic skills and wiring?"

"Well, make sure they attend the training events. Church Volunteer Central has got some great ones," Chris said. "Plus, they have a boatload of other resources, articles, and online forms. Then you'll want to help this person find a network or mentor so that when questions come up, he or she will have someone to talk to who's got some experience."

Matt made notes on his laptop. "What's the Web site for Church Volunteer Central?"

"It's www.churchvolunteercentral.com," Chris said.

"So what if we can't afford to hire someone like Chris?" Matt asked.

"We couldn't either when we began," Vernon said.

"You still can't afford me," Chris said, laughing at his own joke.

"True," Vernon said, "but there are ways you can esteem a person in this role. Give that person an office, business cards, and official staff status, even if you can't pay them. Make sure they are given the same status as the other staff members, and be sure to include them in the staff meetings as much as possible because the other staff members need to see that you value equipping."

"**D**o you have a written job description?" Matt asked. "That might help me know how to talk to someone about what to expect."

"Oh sure," Vernon said. "Actually, we call them ministry descriptions and everyone in a role of service has one."

Matt laughed as in disbelief.

"I'll go get a copy," Chris said, heading for the office door.

"Everyone at Westover has a ministry description?" Matt asked.

"Everyone in a service role, sure. Do you have one?" Vernon asked.

Matt was silent. "Well, come to think of it, no."

"I recently read an article in Rev! Magazine that reported over 70 percent of pastors don't have a written ministry description. What was even more interesting, most of them didn't want one!"

"Really?! Why do you think that is?" Matt said.

"I don't know, but I think it's potentially dangerous," Vernon said. "First of all, how do people know what to expect or how to help the pastor be accountable? Nearly every other professional position has a written job description, including multibillion-dollar corporation CEOs. No pastor should be above healthy accountability, for both encouragement and to help stay focused."

"I never thought of it that way," Matt said. "I guess everyone is assuming a lot."

"That's my point. The second reason it's dangerous is because we tend to revert to the traditional mind-set that assumes the pastor will do it all. This lends itself to inadequate boundaries, which in turn makes a pastor vulnerable to burnout, temptation, and an unhealthy lifestyle," Vernon said.

Matt nodded thoughtfully. "I can see that," he said. "So you have a ministry description?"

"I do," Vernon said. "It's in the same format as everyone else's, whether you're an unpaid nursery worker or full-time, paid, worship team leader. Obviously, mine is described in broader terms than others, as lead pastor, but it's not significantly different than anyone else's in our congregation."

"Here it is," Chris said, re-entering the office. "I also included a couple of samples of other ministry roles here so you can see the format we use." He handed a few sheets of paper to Matt, who began looking them over.

"So you have something like this for everyone involved in service?" Matt asked again, reviewing the document.

"That's right. In fact, that's one of our responsibilities as an equipping team," Chris explained. "We work with existing ministries to help them clarify what type of role they need filled. That helps us match the right people with the right roles."

"What do you mean?" Matt asked.

"I mean there are no wrong people, just wrong roles," Chris explained. "When we put ministry tasks in front of people, we tend to use people. When they don't perform as we'd like, we feel disappointed in them. This creates both obvious and unconscious resentment, which strains relationships and causes people to feel unappreciated. Many churches lose people who rotate out of ministry, never to return, because they did a lousy job helping people find a place of significance that matched their gifts from the start."

"Good point, Chris," Vernon said, reaching for his paper pad. "We look at it this way." He drew a large triangle on the page, with three lines across it, and wrote some words on the lines.

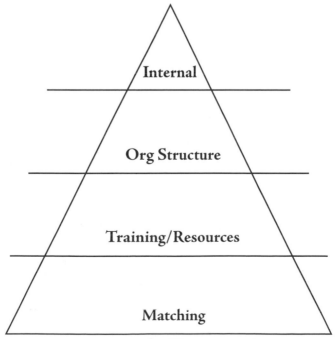

"Instant PowerPoint," Matt said, smiling.

"That's right," Vernon said. "OK, here." He pointed to the bottom section, labeled *matching*. "When a person fails to succeed in a ministry role, the number one reason is because we've done an inadequate job connecting a person to the right role. You have to think: There are no wrong people, only wrong positions. Therefore, until you have a specific role and break it into qualities, skills, and aptitudes, you'll have a difficult time knowing who to look for."

"It's kind of like eHarmony for ministry," Chris said. "If you want a good ministry match, you need to know about the characteristics of the service role as well as the person."

"That's right. Describe the role and help the person discover his or her gifts. A distant second in terms of a good match is having adequate *training and resources*," Vernon said, pointing to the next tier from the bottom on the triangle. "How many times do we in the church get desperate for a Sunday school teacher, find a warm body, toss them a teacher's guide, and say 'God bless you'?"

"Quite often, I guess," Matt said.

"You know it," Vernon said. "And then we wonder why we have so much turnover, or why people don't seem to respond to a teacher's teaching and grow spiritually. The church is about the only organization where you can have a role of influence with practically no training. Shame on us for lowering the bar so much that quality people don't want to apply. On top of that, we fail to help people develop their gifts. We set them up to fail."

"Ouch! I resemble that remark."

"The third reason people fail in a service role is *org. structure*," Vernon explained.

"What do you mean by that?" Matt asked.

"It could be any number of things. Often it's a lack of accountability and feedback structure within the church as an organization," Vernon said. "All of us work better if we have a healthy system where we're held accountable and feel a part of the team. We used to do an annual strategic planning event for our staff and board, but after awhile we noticed people weren't participating. When we began asking them 'why,' we realized they'd become cynical; after the retreat, we rarely ever implemented what we'd invested our time planning. As a result of that feedback, we changed how we do things."

Vernon continued. "Sometimes, it's just a matter of organizational dysfunction in general, where we ask people to do things but then don't trust them or empower them to succeed. For example, we used to run a big Family Fun Day every spring. It was a pretty big deal, run by volunteers. But in order for them to spend money, they had to go through a ridiculous budget permission process or have all sorts of red tape in getting reimbursed. Our concern for financial accountability in this area had gotten out of hand, so that we were conveying the idea that 'We don't trust you.' We wondered why we couldn't get quality people to run the event, until we uncovered what was wrong."

"Uncovering organizational factors can be difficult," Vernon noted, "but sometimes bylaws, denominational controls, and church governance can create significant roadblocks without us realizing what's wrong. Chances are if you can't seem to put your finger on what's holding you back, and you keep running into a wall, there's something wrong structurally."

Matt looked down at his notes.

"I'll give you this sheet when I'm done," Vernon said. "Now, the final reason people fail in a ministry role tends to be *internal issues*." He pointed to the top of the triangle. "This might be irresponsibility, a lack of commitment, family dilemmas, sin, or personality issues. Think about it: When someone fails in a ministry, where do we usually start in terms of blame?"

Matt looked at Vernon's graphic. "More than likely we question a person's character," he said, pointing to the top of the triangle.

Vernon laughed. "You're right, brother. The first thing we do is blame people for being fickle or uncommitted or even carnal. But when you look at the primary causes for ministry malfunction, who is responsible for these first three tiers?"

"Leaders and staff, I suppose," Matt said.

"Right again," Vernon said. "So when people don't work out as we planned, we should first look in the mirror and ask 'How did I fail this person?' not 'Why did they fail me?' Our goal is to help people succeed, to help them not fail. We all do better with wins under our belt."

"Wow, I bet that would help us from getting jaded in the ministry," Matt said. "But isn't it intimidating for people to have a ministry description? You know, like they're being saddled with one more job?"

"Actually, it's just the opposite," Chris said. "A written ministry description, describing the tasks, estimated time requirements, training requirements, resources, and expectations, along with qualifications, actually helps people make commitments."

"Really?" Matt asked.

"Yes, because it says, 'We take this role seriously enough to describe it to you, and you know what you're getting into.' Sometimes people don't commit because ministry can become a black hole that sucks people into things they regret," Chris said. "People actually respond more readily now than they did before we had them."

"Plus a ministry description is a great communication tool," Vernon added. "It helps clarify what we need, thus cutting down on misunderstandings and conflict. Most conflict is a matter of unmet expectations."

"Like what?" Matt asked.

"For example, if you expect a board member to tithe, to attend a small group, to be in regular worship attendance three out of four weeks per month, and maintain certain personal lifestyle standards, then you'd better be clear about that. Don't assume what's in your mind is in their minds. If you're thinking one thing but the board members are thinking differently, tension begins to build. You start feeling frustrated. The board members sense that but don't say anything, which causes your relationship to be strained."

"Sounds a lot like marriage," Matt said, jokingly.

Vernon laughed. "Bingo! Same thing. It's tough to do ministry together when you've set yourself up to have conflict—that's why you've got to clearly communicate mutual expectations up front. Nothing creates clarity like putting it in writing. It's not a contract; it's a communication tool."

"That makes so much sense," Matt said. "Did you come up with these ministry descriptions on your own or is there a place that lists them?"

"You don't need to start from scratch," Chris said. "You can get a lot of them at Church Volunteer Central and then edit them to fit your specific needs. I can also give you a list of equipping churches in our network that are willing to share their ideas and resources."

"That'd be great," Matt said. "Wow, I asked for a single job description and I got all this."

"We're here to serve," Vernon said, smiling at the young pastor.

"**V**ernon, as you look back, what would you say is the biggest challenge that surprised you?" Matt asked. "You know, something you weren't expecting when you tried to live out this equipping value."

"Hmm? Interesting question. I'd say the biggest challenge or surprise wasn't the congregation's lack of embracing the value. It was the staff's," Vernon said.

"Really?" Matt asked in disbelief.

"Yup. We got a lot of pushback from staff. They didn't like the idea of having a less upfront role. They had a hard time with the team-training approach for engaging people into ministry. In fact, we eventually had to ask four of them to leave," Vernon said.

"Wow—that seems odd. I guess I figured it would be the congregation that'd balk the most," Matt said. "Why did the staff resist?"

"I suppose it's a variety of things. More than likely, it was something different for each person. Most of them weren't trained in how to equip others. They came aboard when it was the traditional model. The pastor being the center of all ministry, you know? So they assumed their job security was based on their talent and experience, how well they could perform individually. A couple of staff didn't buy into the 'theological' implications, assuming that what they'd experienced as tradition was what Scriptures taught. And for the couple we had to ultimately let go, I think it had become an ego issue. They didn't want to let go of being the person on the platform who had all the answers," Vernon explained.

"Wow, I would never have thought that. So how did you introduce this to your staff initially?"

"We took a lot of time to sort of roll out the vision and the plan. There were no overnight mandates or ultimatums. Speed kills. We offered to send them to training events that Group Publishing put on for equipping or to get coaching skills, but a few of them resisted all the way to the end. When we saw that the two were just not going to buy in to this paradigm shift, we had to let them go. We gave them a good severance and affirmed them, but you have to get the right people on the bus."

"Jim Collins, *Good to Great?*"

"You got it, Matt," Chris said. "Letting the staff members go made a huge difference to our team, and it also told everyone that we were serious about embracing this value."

"Did that discourage you, the staff resistance?" Matt asked.

"It really did," Vernon answered. "When we read books on team and mobilizing laity and spelled out what Scriptures taught, we assumed that it would make full sense. But I guess it goes back to the reality that change is difficult. People have a hard time rethinking who they are in light of what they do."

"I only have a couple of part-time staff, so I guess I thought that adding staff would be our solution," Matt said.

"Well, it's not a matter of how many staff, but what kind of staff," Chris said.

"So what kind of staff do you look for now?" Matt asked.

Vernon nodded to Chris. "You take this one."

"Ironically, we don't start with ministry talent. We begin with training and team-building skills," Chris said. "These gifts tend to look quite different than typical ministry talent. Plus, we don't just ask them leading questions such as 'Do you do ministry by team?' or 'Do you develop people?' because everyone thinks they do that if they include others in ministry. When we talk about team ministry and developing people, we're talking about this level." Chris held his hand up over his head, gesturing a high standard. "Most staff members are thinking in terms of this level." He lowered his hand to his waist. "We ask, 'Who have you developed as a ministry leader in the last year?' and then we contact those people for feedback on how this person actually equipped. It takes more time, but we've learned that you need to be thorough. It's a lot easier to talk the talk."

"Was there any conflict during the staff transition?" Matt asked.

"One staff member quietly left. Another made a big stink. He tried to rally several people around him and sent a bunch of letters suggesting that what I was doing was not biblical or theologically correct," Vernon said. "I suppose a few people left because of it, but we didn't see any residual effect. For the most part, it's pretty hard to argue against the priesthood of believers when you base it on Scripture. It's the implementation of it that is the sticking point."

"I thought you said you ended up letting four people go," Matt said. "You only mentioned two."

"I'm sorry, you're right," Vernon said. "Those two were pastoral staff. But we also had a few trials in the area of our ministry assistants."

"Who are they?" Matt asked.

"We refer to our administrative support people as ministry assistants," Vernon said.

"I don't understand. Why would they be upset about an equipping ministry?" Matt asked. "Did they have to do more coordinating or something?"

"No, actually it was because we also expected them to model equipping," Vernon said. "We made it a part of their job description to oversee volunteers in the area of their work."

"Really?" Matt said.

"We said if this is going to be a churchwide value, then paid ministry assistants needed to have their own team members," Vernon said. "Several of them were pretty upset with this at the beginning."

"Why?" Matt asked.

"After some heart-to-heart talks, we discovered that they were worried about losing their jobs," Vernon said. "They thought that if they trained unpaid team members to do what they did, we wouldn't need them anymore and think we could get by with volunteers."

"So does your ministry assistant practice team ministry?" Matt asked.

"Absolutely. In fact, she tries to model it for everyone. She oversees four teams of volunteers who do a variety of things," Vernon said.

"Such as what?" Matt asked.

"One team gathers all the details for hospital calls, so that when I make a phone call to someone in the hospital I know their spouse's name and if they're in a small group or ministry. One group transcribes all my messages into written form. Another team writes short, daily devotionals we send out each week, based on the theme of my message. One other team does things such as filing and office tasks," Vernon explained.

"Wow, that's a lot of people," Matt said.

"Look at all we accomplish that we couldn't with a single, paid ministry assistant," Vernon said.

"That makes sense," Matt said. "I'm still trying to get my mind around it."

"Since the transition, we've worked hard at finding staff who are equippers and team-builders. Often that means hiring from within because you mine a lot of untapped potential when you do this. Plus you discover people who have a heart for doing ministry the way you do, who are willing to donate their time and even take drastic salary reductions in order to become a part of the church staff," Chris said.

"Wow, that is interesting," Matt said. "About what percent of your staff is hired from within?"

"Oh, probably 70 percent," Chris said. "The rule of thumb is that if a ministry is going well, hire from within. If changes need to be made, then usually it's best to bring in someone from the outside, as they tend to bring new ideas. Plus, they are unfamiliar with whatever sacred cows or political alliances exist and tend to go around them or confront them. They come with fresh eyes."

"That's so different from the traditional approach of trying to bring in the best and brightest talent from the outside," Matt said.

"Well, it's not that you want untalented people," Vernon said, laughing. "It's just that you want the right kind of talent. Ministry doers tend to want to build the team around themselves, which in turn makes it very difficult when they leave. Plus, it diminishes the number of people we have in a ministry, which lessens the ownership and thus commitment. We're significantly understaffed compared to most churches our size, but that gives us more budget for programming, outreach, and resourcing our unpaid staff. In fact, we actually have paid support staff who serve unpaid leaders. How about that?"

"Wow, that is amazing, but it really makes sense," Matt said. "So how do you know if your paid staff are doing their job as equippers?"

"We include it in their ministry description, as well as their semiannual reviews," Vernon said. "When salary and promotions—not to mention your job longevity—are attached to how many people you've developed, it says you're committed to making it happen. You can expect what you inspect."

"Plus, we're frequently analyzing what ministries are well-staffed and which ones seem understaffed," Chris added. "We periodically survey team members to see how they're doing, plus we provide confidential feedback questionnaires to see how they feel their leader is doing in developing the team."

"Wow, so you're not the only ones analyzing staff, huh?" Matt asked.

"No," Vernon said. "Whether we like it or not, we're all being analyzed all the time, but when you gather feedback that you can use for improving team leaders, then it becomes constructive and helpful. We try to leverage input from team members."

"You've given me a lot to think about, but it's also nice to hear that it's not all rosy in terms of making it happen," Matt said.

"Not at all," Chris said. "There is a price to be paid…"

"That's what Vernon told me," Matt interrupted.

"And it's well worth the investment," Chris added.

The Equipping Team

"I've got to run to a lunch with a couple of our new board members—leadership development," Vernon said. "Chris, why don't you have Matt sit in your equipping ministry lunch meeting so he can see how your team functions; that is, if Matt doesn't have other plans."

"No, that would be great," Matt said.

"Super," Chris responded. "Then we can talk about it afterward."

"You'll enjoy seeing how Chris works with this team," Vernon said. The senior pastor excused himself from the office, and Chris led Matt down the hall to a meeting room. A man and woman were arranging food and drinks on a table.

"Hey, Ian and Suzi, how are you?" Chris said, shaking hands with the older couple. "That looks wonderful. What do you have today for us?"

"Oh, we've got some cold cuts, salad, and soft drinks," the woman responded, smiling.

"And some of Suzi's brownies," Ian said. "Might look quite nice on that trim waist of yours, Chris," Ian said, patting his own stomach.

"That's what I'm afraid of. Those brownies are addictive," Chris said. "Hey, I want you to meet a friend of mine, Pastor Matt Robinson. He's the pastor over at Crossroads Church."

Matt talked with Ian and Suzi as other members of the equipping team trickled into the room. Chris introduced each one to Matt, making him feel welcome. After lunch Chris led a devotional about servant leadership from John 13, about Jesus washing his disciples' feet. Chris brought in a warm bowl of water and a white washcloth. He dipped the washcloth into the bowl and went around to each of the eight people in the room and wiped their hands. Matt felt the honor and embarrassment when Chris ran the warm cloth over his hands. He could tell that the others in the group seemed touched by the devotional. The lesson only took 10 minutes, but it set the tone for the rest of the hour meeting.

A woman named Elizabeth led the meeting. "All right, how's everyone doing in their area of ministry?" Elizabeth asked. "Let's do a brief check in, and then we have three short agenda items we need to discuss before we get you back to work or the golf course or whatever you're up to today."

Each member of the group gave a brief summary of an area he or she supervised. All but one of them referred to their own ministry team. Matt realized that this was a team of leaders, not so much ministry doers. Team members represented ministry involvement in children and youth, community outreach, worship, small groups, communication, and administration. The agenda items involved discussing plans for a fall ministry fair to promote involvement, reviewing how the *Discovering Your Gifts and Niche* training could be promoted better, and topic themes for the leadership team's upcoming retreat.

The meeting adjourned almost to the minute noted on the agenda. Matt and Chris walked down the hall from the meeting room to Chris' office. "Any thoughts or suggestions for us?" Chris asked, motioning to a chair for Matt. "Here, have a seat."

"Thanks," Matt responded. "No, I'm making all these mental notes that I can use in running our ministry meeting, but mostly it's good to see how someone like you actually functions. I was impressed that you had lunch, a devotional…"

"Actually, that was more of a leader lesson. We do something like that every time we meet, but it may or may not include Scripture."

"OK, that was good to see, but you stayed right on time."

"We have to because of work schedules. A couple of people were unable to make the meeting, and six of the eight there have full-time jobs."

"I'm impressed that they do this every month."

"Every two weeks, actually. It's a pretty active team, but most of the meetings involve reporting and helping each other trouble-shoot or brainstorm solutions in their area of responsibility. We're fortunate to have a highly committed bunch."

"So I gather that these are not the ministry doers."

"Well, we all do certain things, but more as a 'player coach.' This is my top team, who has teams of their own. We try to live leadership in our church, finding people who can put together a team and then organize it. You can't take this equipping lightly if it's going to work. There are far too many details and people. As you know, it takes a lot of time for planning, listening, communicating, relationship building, working through conflict, some counseling, and just hanging out together."

"I'm feeling very overwhelmed right about now," Matt said, wiping his brow.

"You're looking at an evolution," Chris laughed. "We've been doing this now for just short of a decade, but it wasn't always this finely tuned, and—to be honest—we're always either repairing or changing things, so don't let me give you the impression that we've got it all together."

"Yes, but I guess I had some weird idea that you, because you're full-time, just sort of did it yourself."

"If we're moving away from a pastor-centric ministry model, only to replace it with a staff-centric ministry, that wouldn't make sense, would it?"

"No, it certainly wouldn't."

"I have to work as a team just as Vernon and the other ministry staff members do, which is why at Vernon's level, developing leaders occupies nearly all his time outside of his sermon prep, and even that is now done more by team than ever before. This gives him more time to prepare leader lessons and disciple potential leaders around Westover."

Partner as Champion

"I'm curious, though, to know more about how you interact with the lead pastor in your role," Matt said.

"OK, shoot," Chris said. "What do you mean?"

"Oh, you know, how you help him stay focused on elevating the equipping value when he's being pulled in other directions."

"Ah, yes, that can be a challenge. Of course it's much easier now that it's become a part of our culture at Westover. Getting started was difficult for us."

"I mean, he called you a partner, but we all know that regardless of how much we promote servant leading, there's an authority issue here, in that he's the leader and you're the staff member. How do you know when to push?"

"Well, let me give you some examples. We use the word *champion* sometimes around here. We're not talking about competition or super-achievers but rather *champion* as a verb. I'm to champion the value of equipping throughout the church. That means my responsibility is also to hold Vernon accountable. He's charged me to do that. I think that you, as pastor, have to give both permission and authority to your equipping director to raise concerns or suggestions he or she has in this area. Obviously, for any partnership, there has to be mutual trust. Remember, I didn't start in a paid role, so I didn't have anything to lose in speaking my mind. I'd suggest you empower your partner to do that if you're serious about equipping. That can be embarrassing at times. Ego checks always are, but again, this is a team approach—we're colleagues in ministry."

"What do you mean 'ego checks,' Chris? Vernon strikes me as one of the most humble leaders I've ever met."

"Oh, he is, but he's also human. We all are. As pastors, we often think we know more, that we speak for God, and that our decisions are the best. That's human. But being open to feedback, even when it contradicts these emotions, can be awkward. At the start, Vernon and I met weekly to go over strategy, talk philosophy, and he coached me."

"So he trusted you?"

"That's imperative. But part of my job is to help see that he embodies the equipping value. For example, one time I had to sit down with him and in essence say, 'Vernon, you've got to quit doing hospital calls.' He enjoyed that traditional pastoral role, but he was telegraphing the idea that this was a pastoral duty, instead of equipping others with gifts of mercy and shepherding to use them. Another time I had to ask him to reconsider having newcomers over to his home. I said, 'Let those with gifts of hospitality do that. If you're going to open up your home, do it for leaders and those you want to develop as leaders.' It's a matter of thinking and behaving differently."

"Wow, that's interesting. So what do you do when you sense the vision is weakening?"

"Well again, early on, I used to ask if I could see in advance what he was preaching on, to see if I might brainstorm some ways that he could subtly convey the equipping value in messages. A pastor can sabotage what you're trying to do in just a few words from the pulpit. On a couple of occasions, I'd go up to him between services and ask him if he'd consider modifying an illustration or comment."

"Wow, that's pretty gutsy. We preachers don't take kindly to people meddling in our messages."

"It was a bit awkward at the moment, but he thanked me afterward, because there was trust between us, and he was open to seeing how he could help our church embrace this value."

"What else is important for a pastor to know about working with a partner? Partner? Is there another word for this role?"

Chris laughed. "Yeah, it's really just a good way to describe the relationship with the pastor, but we've had half a dozen titles, and I've heard another dozen used in other churches. 'Director of equipping ministry' or 'ministry involvement,' 'spiritual gifts director,' 'pastor of service,' and 'assimilation coordinator' are titles we've used in the past. Some churches are recognizing the power of discipleship, so a few are using 'pastor of discipleship' as a title for the equipping champion."

"So how else do you and Vernon work together?"

"Well, sometimes I'll ask his help in matters because he is seen as the leader of our church. For example, even when I was unpaid, he invited me to all the pastoral staff meetings because he wanted to make sure that I was seen as a peer and to make sure lines of communication were open. This helped convey that equipping should be a part of every ministry in the church."

"Did staff accept this?"

"At first they sort of wondered why I was there, but when the lead pastor supports you, it gets the point across. One time, we were trying to get all the staff and ministry leaders involved in our annual ministry fair, where we showcase service opportunities inside and outside the church. The event got pushback by the staff, who felt they were busy with their individual ministries and didn't feel the need to prioritize involvement personally or by their team representatives. I asked Vernon if he'd convey the importance of this.

"We had a staff leadership retreat and one of the sessions involved Vernon informing all the staff that they were expected to be involved in this churchwide event. When the lead pastor says things, it tends to have greater buy-in from the staff than if I tried to convince them on my own. Vernon has always been an ally and advocate, and I appreciate that about him."

"I like it. I like this whole idea of not being alone in ministry. I like the idea that it doesn't rest on my shoulders, but that I can be an advocate for the equipping champion. I can do this."

"Sure you can, Matt. It won't be easy, but it's the right thing to do. After it becomes a part of your church culture, then you just have to maintain the value, which is actually easier than creating the change initially."

THE
PARTNER

Pastor Coach

After his lunch appointment, Vernon met up with Matt and Chris.

"So what did you think of the meeting?" Vernon asked. "Was it helpful to watch how our equipping team functions a bit?"

"It was great," Matt said. "Funny, I guess I'm still sort of stuck in Pastorville, thinking that the staff members make this happen themselves instead of working together as a team."

"Ah yes," Vernon said. "One of the things we do here a lot is talk team. If you stuck around long enough, you'd discover that the word *I* is rarely used. In fact, it's kind of a bad omen when a new staff member uses that word *I* a lot, because we've found they often don't end up lasting long. Changing that wiring is very difficult for some pastors."

"Do you think it's because there's kind of a fraternity among pastors?" Matt suggested. "I mean, until you've been a senior or solo pastor, I'm not sure if you understand what we feel and go through."

"You're probably right," Vernon said. "I think that can add to the feeling of loneliness and isolation. But I don't think you have to give up the unique sense of being a pastor in order to help develop teams in your church. I've found the less I feel alone and isolated, the more I find people who truly have a pastor's heart, regardless of their training or title. I guess the fraternity of a heart for ministry transcends that of the ordained."

"That's good," Matt said, nodding agreement. "If you don't mind, I'm interested in knowing how you work with Chris, or at least what you go over in your meetings. He was able to tell me his perspective of how you work together."

"Well, we used to meet weekly the first two or three years, but now it's sort of dwindled to once every two weeks, I suppose because we've developed the culture and understand each other's rhythm."

"That's true," Chris said.

"Would you rather we discuss this separately?" Matt asked, thinking there might be some hesitance for Vernon to be open with Chris present.

"Oh, not at all," Vernon said. "We're very open with each other and have developed a pretty strong sense of trust between us by now. That's essential if you're going to make a paradigm shift in this direction. Well, what do you think, Chris? What do you find helpful in our meetings?"

"To be honest, I like the way you coach," Chris said.

"What do you mean 'coach'?" Matt asked. "You mentioned it before, but what does that look like on a regular basis?"

"It looks like not telling me what to do or giving me answers to the problems that I raise," Chris said. "A good coach recognizes the benefit of helping someone wrestle through a process so that he or she is more capable as a result. When you merely provide an opinion or an answer, you're not really developing staff."

"Any examples?" Matt asked.

"Why don't we actually discuss our upcoming service weekend?" Vernon said. "We were going to talk about that anyway."

"OK," Chris said. "Well, we're about six months away from our Serve Pleasant Valley weekend, where hundreds of our people gather for a full day of working on schools, shut-ins' homes, and fix-it projects for the needy in PV and the surrounding area. A couple of ideas are to make it a bigger thrust or emphasis by canceling our weekend services, and secondly, inviting other churches to join us, so it's not just a Westover event."

"Let's take one idea at a time," Vernon said. "What do you think about shutting down our weekend services?"

"Well, there are pros and cons," Chris said. "Obviously, it eases up the time impact on families, who might feel pressure to do a whole workday and then come to church either as a participant or a worker or both."

"Good point. What else?" Vernon said.

"I think that by canceling, or rather exchanging our services, it makes a big statement in terms of priority. We're saying that serving is a form of worship, and I think it would be a great statement of our faith," Chris said.

"Are there any examples of churches who've done this we might learn from?" Vernon asked.

"I've read about a couple of churches, one in southern California and one in northern California that have done this. Rock Harbor in Orange County, I think, and Menlo Park Presbyterian Church did it," Chris said.

"Were they positive experiences?" Vernon asked.

"I think so, but let me follow up with phone calls so I can get more details," Chris said, making a note on his PDA.

"What's the possible downside of doing this?" Vernon asked.

"Well, you're going to have some traditionalists who will be upset, who'll criticize this or even go to another church that Sunday," Chris said. "You're also likely to lose some possible visitors who show up expecting a church service but find everyone gone."

"That might be positive, too, I suppose, if someone is here to explain what we're doing," Vernon said.

"Plus you have the possibility of getting media exposure and the impact in the community, so that more people end up visiting Westover," Chris added.

"What about the offering?" Vernon said. "If there's no offering, what kind of impact do you think that might make on our budget?"

"I've thought about that," Chris asked. "I'll ask those churches when I contact them, but I think that if we budget in advance for a lower weekend and let people know in advance that they can drop off their offering before, during, or after, that might help. Plus, we might even have some extra gifts from folks who like the idea of a church prioritizing service over 'serve-us,' at least one weekend."

"OK," Vernon said, "why don't you do a little more homework, and we'll talk about it before bringing it up with some of our board members."

Vernon and Chris continued this sort of conversation for another half-hour, expanding the talk about shutting down weekend services as well as discussing partnering with other churches in the area. At the end of the meeting, Chris had written a list of about five or six action steps that he was going to follow up on before their next meeting in two weeks.

At the culmination of the conversation, Vernon said, "So that was pretty typical of one of our meetings. Obviously, some meetings are more of a check in, and others are more strategic like this one, but the feel is similar."

"That's true," Chris said.

"So Vernon doesn't have all the answers for you?" Matt asked.

"To be honest, he rarely does; but I can tell if he's not satisfied with my solutions because he'll continue asking me more probing questions. Or he'll get me to consider alternative ideas," Chris said.

"Coaching is a helpful skill for pastors," Vernon said, "because it doesn't require me to have all the answers, and it develops our staff so they're more self-sufficient and proficient."

"Plus it's a good way to model how Vernon wants all leaders to function at Westover," Chris said. "We try to operate from a team approach."

"**I** keep hearing about this 'team' thing," Matt said. "Help me understand that better. What's the difference between a team and a committee? I get the feeling that with all the hype about teams in the corporate world, that all of a sudden we want to be hip in the church, so we start referring to our committees as teams. I guess being in an independent church, we've tried to avoid having a lot of bureaucracy and committees. So I don't want to start them and call them teams, if this is a fad."

Vernon laughed. "I don't blame you, man. Committees nearly killed our church. The big difference between 'committees' and 'teams' is that most teams are action-oriented and only function when there is something to be accomplished. Committees tend to be ongoing and are less action-oriented, more managerial, and maintenance-oriented. Probably the only committee-type group we have at Westover is the church board, and even then we're pretty tight in terms of action steps and follow-up."

"There are a lot of good resources out there to help you think team instead of committee," Chris said. "Wayne Cordiero has a good book called *Doing Church As a Team*, but to be honest, most of our resources have come from the business community such as Patrick Lencioni's *The Five Dysfunctions of a Team*. We also brought in Nancy Ortberg and Tammy Kelly to do some consulting for us as well, but there's no reason any church can't begin thinking team ministry versus individualistic ministry."

"Although it sounds un-American, it is certainly more biblical and global in style," Vernon said. "Pastor-centric ministry uses people to support clergy, while teams tend to be strategic, sharing involvement and ownership. This is far more egalitarian, but that's what equipping requires.

"That reminds me, Chris," Vernon continued. "A while back, Matt asked me about the differences in how we use the terms *equip, develop,* and *train*. Could you make a note to make sure we clarify these among our key leaders? We might want to work on that a bit. We're always trying to improve things. It's a constant."

"Good idea," Chris said, tapping the keys of his PDA.

"You young guys and your electronic toys," Vernon said, motioning to Chris. "You run circles around me."

Chris shrugged his shoulders. "Hey, if sundials and flannel board work for you, more power to you."

The men laughed. "Oops, I need to slip out to another meeting," Chris said. "Matt, great being with you today. I look forward to us spending more time together. Let me know if I can include any of your people in our training and mentoring process. We've been doing this the last two or three years for other churches. We have everyone sign an 'I'll remain in my own church' agreement so it can be as safe as possible for you to trust our motives."

"Wow, that's great. Thanks so much," Matt said, shaking hands with Chris as he left.

"I can't get over how helpful you are, sharing what you've learned with others," Matt said. "I have to admit, I haven't always felt that supportive of you, being the big church on the block and all."

"Well, I guess when you take on an equipping mentality it just overflows into other areas, like feeling less competition with other churches and doing whatever we can to strike strategic partnerships. We're all on the same team. We're just called to different positions."

"I sense that from you. You mentioned that if you had it to do over again, you'd have brought on a director of equipping much sooner. What other things would you recommend for getting going?"

"I think the biggest single issue is the conviction. The conviction that this really is the right way to pastor, to implement Ephesians 4 throughout the church. Like we said from the start, if you're just looking for a slick way to recruit more workers, that's not enough to shift the paradigm. Once you have that conviction, then you begin in incremental ways. For example, in the past, at the end of my messages, we invited people to come forward to make a decision of faith. Traditionally, a pastor or pastoral staff member would meet people down front. But I began training people who had a heart for sharing their faith and praying with people. So when people came forward after my invitation, someone from this ministry team would meet them, not just me or a staff member."

"Here's another thing," Vernon continued. "We establish this value very clearly in our membership class."

"Do you teach that yourself?"

"I teach this part, where I let people know that part of their spiritual growth involves service. At one point I pass out puzzle pieces of a 6-foot-tall picture of Jesus and ask them to stick their piece up on the wall, anywhere. It's usually quite a mess. Then I say, 'This is the body of Christ when we aren't using our gifts together.' Then we put the pieces together so they can see what it was intended to be by design. It makes quite a visual point. Then I tell them that if they're not ready to get involved in some sort of active service, then membership is not right for them at this time, but when they're ready to serve, join us."

"Wow! Does that scare people away?"

"Not as much as you'd think. We usually have about 80 percent join at that point, but we've established our expectations. It seems to work best after they've taken the course called *Finding Your Niche*. Chris and his staff teach this and explain the process of discovering and using your gifts. Education really is important to make sure people understand this value in your church."

Matt put his laptop in his computer bag and stood to leave. "Thanks so much, Vernon. Today was really helpful. I feel overwhelmed with new ideas. I'm going to have to percolate on these awhile."

"See, even your verbs sound like coffee-making. Percolate awhile, but we're going to see you tonight at the board meeting, aren't we?"

"Oh that's right. I'll be there. It'll be nice to share someone else's pain."

"Oh I don't know. We have a pretty good time in our board meetings. We'll see you later."

Board Meeting

"I've invited a guest to join us tonight," Vernon said, introducing Matt to Westover's church board members. The men and women greeted Matt genuinely, and the two pastors sat along the side of the table. Vernon began with a devotion on leadership from the book of Nehemiah, concluding with a five-minute leader lesson activity, which really seemed to pique conversation among the members.

"Do you do this every meeting?" Matt whispered to Vernon, as the group got settled around the table again.

"Every time," Vernon said. "That's my job, to be the chief spiritual officer and leadership developer."

Matt leaned back and turned toward Vernon, assuming he'd chair the remainder of the meeting. But to his surprise, neither Vernon nor the executive pastor spoke next. A medium-build, sharp-looking businessman sitting at the end of the table began facilitating the agenda. The remainder of the meeting was vibrant, focusing on governance issues, with most matters being assigned to ministry teams, including action steps and time deadlines. As the meeting was coming to a close, Matt looked down at his watch. *Wow, 9 p.m.*, he thought. *That was a fast, productive meeting. I wish more of our board meetings at Crossroads got that much accomplished in two hours.*

After people chatted farewells, Matt and Vernon walked out to the parking lot together.

"So what did you think?" Vernon asked.

"Is that a typical board meeting?" Matt replied.

"Pretty much. Obviously, issues vary from month to month. Occasionally we'll call a special meeting if there's a pressing issue. But since most of our members coordinate areas they oversee, our board meetings tend to be more reporting and some wrestling with issues pertaining to the whole church."

"Wow, that's impressive. How long did it take you to turn over the meeting to a layperson?"

"Well, first of all, I'm from a mainline tradition so there's a precedent for the pastor not being the board chair; but even then, I used to run my own meetings. But one time, at a retreat, I asked one of our members to facilitate the discussion. He did an amazing job, and several commented how much they enjoyed the meeting. I caught on quickly that maybe there was someone better at running meetings."

"So even though you're the pastor, you let others oversee the business matters?"

"The ongoing daily matters are overseen by paid staff, but we always keep a few unpaid businesspeople on the action team so that they can pushback on our practices and ask strategic questions. But our board meetings are more about reporting and policy matters."

"I was taught to believe that was my job. You know, to run board meetings."

"I came to realize that I'm called to be a pastor. I'm not a businessman. If God had made me that way, I'd be in the marketplace. Why would I want to try to lead my church organizationally, when I've got far more competent and experienced people who do this every day of their lives? I'd be embarrassed, because while I'm trying to muddle through an agenda dealing with budgets or staffing or facilities or growth, I know the professionals would be thinking to themselves, *This guy is clueless.* But more important, I'd be diminishing the effectiveness of Westover organizationally. The man who led tonight is an entrepreneur whose company is 10 times larger than our church. He's making strategic decisions every day in his business, while I'm hunkered away in my study, coming up with God's message for our congregation this week. He's good at what he does, so why not tap his experience?"

"Good point. I remember taking a practical ministry course in seminary, where we learned how to run a church board meeting. Notice I said 'we' learned how to run a board meeting. No one ever told us it might make more sense to have a savvy businessperson run it."

"Been there, done that."

Finding Leaders

"**S**o how do you find the influencers in your church?" Matt asked. "As I look at our church, I think some of the people on our board are well-intended but not necessarily the strongest leaders."

"Good observation," Vernon replied. "My experience tells me that in many churches, some of the best leaders are not on the boards or in charge of ministries. Part of the reason is that they're busy. But I've found that busy people make time for what they find fulfilling and meaningful. The bigger issue is that pastors fail to identify the strongest leaders or they're intimidated by them. Like attracts like. If you begin to have non-leaders on the board or in key ministry roles, then other leaders are less apt to be involved because they get frustrated with the process and thinking of non-leaders."

"So how do you identify these people?"

"I look for four things. First, I look for people who lead in the marketplace. Society has a way of elevating those with leadership gifts. I'm not necessarily talking about people who own their own business and only oversee a few people. I'm looking for folk who supervise other adults, cast vision, and have some accomplishments under their belts."

Matt began writing notes on the back of a brochure he'd picked up in the church lobby.

Vernon held up two fingers. "Second, I interview them and listen for a track record of leadership situations, such as being the student body president, or team captain of the basketball team, or being promoted to VP after a short time on the job. Let others do the dirty work of testing your candidate.

"Three," Vernon continued, "I observe who is missed when they're gone and who is listened to when they talk. Everyone isn't created equal when it comes to influence. Certain people are noticed by their absence or their presence. I look for individuals who other people ask about, want their opinions in meetings, or tend to gravitate toward. Most leaders have an air about them."

"What's the fourth?"

"If possible, I give potential leaders a project to do that requires organizational and team skills. The church ought to be an incubator for leaders, a safe place where we give people a chance to fail or succeed in endeavors. Leaders don't need all the details. They just want to know the goal, the budget, and the timeline. Then they're all over it. When someone ends up doing a ministry task on their own, or complains about burning out, or keeps bugging you with details and questions, or just drops the ball—that's not your person. Thank them. Bless them for volunteering, but make a mental note to self, 'not a strong leader.'"

"You're OK with letting them fail?"

"Was Jesus? Can you say, 'Peter'?"

Matt laughed as Vernon continued. "You have to get used to feeling uncomfortable because that's our job, to give people opportunities to develop and reveal their influence gifts. Bottom line is that if someone thinks he's a leader but no one's following…"

"Then he's just taking a walk," Matt completed Vernon's sentence. "I read Maxwell, too."

"After a while, you begin to get a feel of who is and who isn't a strong leader. Most leaders don't flock. They tend not to ask to be involved, at least not the ones you want. They're also not likely to volunteer or sign a response card after a plea for help. You have to go after them one by one, look them in the eyes and say, 'We need someone of your capacity because we've got big dreams.'"

"So what if you have someone like that who isn't strong spiritually?"

"Ah, well that's why we're pastors, isn't it? Our job is to prepare the saints for works of service, which in the context of church leadership means discipleship. Our job is to ground them spiritually so they're prepared to use their influence gifts in the local congregation. For me, it usually involves an ongoing group of four to eight people with whom I meet biweekly, for a leadership Bible study where there's accountability and face time. When I sense they're ready, then I invite them to a modest leadership role, and if they do well there, invite them to do more. It's tedious, but it works. Developing leaders is what I do well, but to be honest, I'm not the strongest leader myself. Maybe that's what Jesus meant when he told his disciples, 'greater things than these' you'll do."

"That was worth the price of admittance. Thanks. I think I need to go home and simmer on this."

"A pastor who is equipping always has a farm team he's developing. You don't advertise it or put it in the bulletin. My gut says that the reason the Twelve stayed with Jesus when his teachings got tough was because he invited them personally. That's a big difference in terms of commitment and longevity."

Control Freak

The next Saturday morning, Vernon came by Matt and Carmen's house for breakfast. Matt had mentioned Carmen's questions about adopting this different approach to pastoring. He felt like he understood it, but wasn't quite sure how to explain it as clearly to his wife. Vernon offered to share some of his ideas with her.

"I don't know what it is," Matt said, "but Starbucks at home just doesn't have the same taste as it does when the barista pours it. Another cup?" He motioned to Vernon, who was sitting at the kitchen table.

"Just a little more," Vernon said. "Carmen, that was a wonderful breakfast. Thank you for your hospitality. I know I came over to talk shop, but it was nice hearing about your family while we ate."

"Oh, we're honored to have you," Carmen said. "A busy man like you probably doesn't do many house calls. I know you've made a big impact on Matt the last few weeks as you've talked about this new approach to ministry. We talk about it a lot, but I just had some questions. Matt thought you might be able to fill in some blanks. Growing up in a pastor's home, I guess I'm a bit skeptical of tampering with the role of the pastor in the local church."

"I don't blame you," Vernon said, sipping his coffee. "In a way, it's not changing the real goal: growing people. It's just a matter of doing it better. They experience change as well as serve. Like I mentioned to Matt, it's more of a math issue. You're multiplying instead of adding."

"But if a pastor is God's representative to the people, aren't you giving up control?" she asked. "That kind of seems like a dangerous thing to do when so many people have wobbly faith. My experience tells me there are always individuals ready to take over a church, or at least run it their way."

"You mean, give them an inch and they'll take a mile?" Vernon asked.

"Yes. I don't mean to sound paranoid, but growing up in a parsonage makes you unfortunately aware of all the politics and control issues that go on out there," Carmen said.

Vernon gave a soft chuckle. "I know. I've been around long enough to see the sort of ego that drives certain board members, those *Well-Intentioned Dragons*

Marshall Shelley wrote about. They come across so spiritual, but they are divisive and undermining."

"Exactly," Carmen said. "Matt has such a great heart, but he's not seen what some people are capable of doing. I'm just afraid that if he turns more of the leadership over to the congregation, we'll have conflict, power struggles, and perhaps even a split."

"I know this may sound demeaning, but it's not meant to be," Vernon said. "I guess the question is, 'Whose church is Crossroads?' If it's Matt's, then it will probably always be constrained by his ability to keep control. If it's God's, then my recommendation is to pastor more like God seemed to suggest through Moses and Jesus."

Carmen chuckled. "It sounds good. It really does, but I'm not sure it works that simply."

"Ah, but simply does not mean easy," Vernon said. "It is very difficult for most of us pastors to let go of ministry, to empower others to make decisions on their own. If you do that without developing those with leadership gifts, then I agree, you're abdicating responsibility. But if you strategically focus on discipling and embracing leaders, then you leverage trust for the benefit of the church."

"What do you mean?" Matt asked.

"I mean that most pastors acknowledge other dominant gifts than leadership. You've read Barna and others who suggest that. That's OK, because you see, God has put enough leadership horsepower in every church. In most churches it doesn't reside in the pastor. That means you have to lead with other people's influence. I call it backseat leading," Vernon said.

"You mean like backseat driving," Matt said, smiling at Carmen.

"All right," Carmen said. "Go on, Vernon."

"Crossroads is an independent church. But Westover was a pretty traditional, mainline church when I came. It had all the governing boards and committees you could ever dream of…or have nightmares about. But regardless of church policy and structure, a pastor has the ability of moving forward, so long as you understand who the influencers are, disciple them spiritually, and then engage them in the planning and decision-making process. It's not easy, but it really is quite simple."

"I've been to some of these teaching church conferences where the pastors say that you're to be the visionary, take-charge, grab-the-bull-by-the-horns leader," Matt said. "I'm just not that kind of guy. I admire those guys, but I go home and think, *If I tried to do that, I'd look like an idiot.*"

Vernon laughed. "I know. I felt the same way. But if you get behind the scenes in some of those churches, you'll find that the senior pastor is more of a despot than he is a servant leader. He's very controlling, but on a grander scale. I began to realize that by trying to control too much, I was holding back our church."

"How'd you let go responsibly?" Matt asked.

"Ah, that's the key: responsibly. As a good steward, you need to let go. Jesus taught 'unless the seed falls into the ground and dies,' 'don't bury your talent,' and 'to whom much is given, much is required.' It all comes down to shrewd, savvy stewardship, doesn't it? The best way to enhance your power is to empower others. Other people must become your partners in ministry. A partner is a helpmate, like both of you. Carmen has unique gifts, abilities, and wiring. Matt, you have unique gifts, abilities, and wiring. As you know, for your marriage to work, you have to have give and take. If someone tries to be too controlling, then you cease to be as effective as you could be together."

Vernon paused, wanting to make sure that his friends were tracking with him.

Letting Go

"**E**phesians 4 talks about the unity all Christians have in the body of Christ. Then it says, 'each has been given different gifts.'" Vernon reached for his leather-bound paper pad, began writing, and continued. "Here. It's like this. We're all together, many yet one. Then it says we're all different because of our various gifts. But when we use our gifts, we mature and become unified. So it looks kind of like this." Vernon turned the paper so that Matt and Carmen could see it better.

"But here's what happens in the typical church," Vernon pointed out. "We have all these gifts and needs and opportunities, but so many of them have to go through the pastor who is trying to control too much. This forms a logjam, which is discouraging to people who want to use their gifts, just as it is frustrating to those whose needs are not being met."

"Looks like a blocked artery," Matt said.

"Exactly; it's organizational heart disease. It leads to hardening of the attitudes, as I like to say."

"But growing up, I've seen my dad run through the wringer," Carmen said. "Have you been hurt deeply by church people, Vernon?"

"Oh, I wish I could say I haven't. You can't be in ministry long without feeling the pain of people you think are friends, who claim to be living with God in them, but who sabotage your ideas and plans. They question

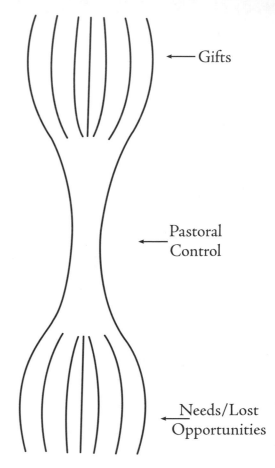

←— Gifts

←— Pastoral Control

←— Needs/Lost Opportunities

your motives, your competency, and your decisions. But what I've discovered is that if I operate out of my hurts and try to control, then I'm ultimately hurting the church and myself. Control is a response to fear of being hurt. Controlling pastors tend to operate out of fear. Church boards that have been injured in their past, more than likely by a pastor, often overcompensate and become controlling.

"Scripture says that love casts out fear. If you're going to lead your church, you're going to have to give up control. It's the only way to let God grow his church into what it was designed to become. To do that, you'll have to become actively involved in the lives of those with influence gifts and abilities, and eventually empower them to join you in the task of leading Crossroads."

"Maybe you're right," Carmen responded. "I don't want to grow old and cynical like so many who've been in ministry."

"It can be a bumpy ride," Vernon encouraged. "But when you look at our Commander and Chief, he pretty much empowered a dozen guys who turned the world upside down. You'll have your detractors. Jesus did. But even then, good can come from bad if you persevere."

"We have to get back to our Model, don't we?" Matt said.

"I still remember when my first son started college. He attends a private Christian university in San Diego. I watched my wife, who has strong nurturing gifts, arranging his room with tender love to help him feel settled. It was her way of getting him ready for life on his own. No matter how much we wanted to stay with him, we had to drive away," Vernon said. "I still tear up a bit, just thinking about it."

"Oh, I'm not looking forward to that day," Carmen said.

"It comes fast," Vernon said, dabbing at the corner of his eye with his finger. "But we had to leave. Cried our brains out as we drove in silence the next hour. There's something so difficult about leaving someone who you've invested so much time, love, and energy in, but our son needed us to do that for him to mature. Since then, he's blossomed."

"We have to get our people ready for us to leave, don't we?" Matt said.

"We do; even if we don't leave our churches, we have to take the attitude of Jesus, who only had a short time before he empowered his congregation to be on their own. Were they ready? Probably not, but that's where the Spirit takes over."

Matt nodded thoughtfully toward Vernon, then looked at Carmen and gave her an encouraging grin.

Vernon continued, "I just think that giving up control and empowering others is the only feasible way to become the church God wants. You just don't want to empower those who are not equipped. That's why equipping is the solution. When a pastor unleashes authority and power to individuals who are ill-equipped or undeveloped, then you're asking for trouble."

"That makes a lot of sense," Matt said. "So this equipping and development are what tends to take place behind the scenes, or at least outside of Sunday morning worship."

"Most of it does," Vernon said. "We do a couple of message series every year, and hardly a Sunday goes by that we don't hear a story or two about people who are using their gifts inside or outside the church. But that's why you need the infrastructure to handle the details of coordinating a whole group of people. It's just too much for any pastor, which is why you need a partner, who will in turn develop a team of folk for this primary purpose."

"It sounds so, so perfect, the way you explain it," Carmen said. "I don't know, I guess I still have to get my arms around the concept."

"Those of us raised in the traditional pastor-centric model have a tough time letting go, but when we do, we begin to see Scripture, ministry, and even our calling in a whole new light. I'd encourage you to keep wrestling with it. We're helping Matt get going with some training and mentoring, but you'll have to figure out what it looks like at Crossroads and with your own gift sets," Vernon said.

"I really appreciate you coming over and helping me think this through a bit," Carmen said. "We see our ministry so much as a partnership, I felt like I needed some processing so I could understand it better and be more supportive."

"No problem," Vernon said. "I'm excited to see how open you are to considering a more effective approach to your ministry. You're both very gifted. I think your best days are just around the corner."

principle

Every church needs a person besides the pastor who will champion the equipping value and develop a ministry team to implement this throughout the ministry areas.

the
PLAN

An Equipping Culture

Two months had gone by since Vernon and Matt had met. They agreed that the time would be well spent for Matt to process what he'd learned. Both pastors had also scheduled family vacations during the summer, which did not overlap. Matt had taken four of the books Vernon mentioned but only got to two of them while he was out of the office. But of the two he read, there were numerous comments in the margins and underlining. A few nights, Matt and Carmen stayed up after the kids were asleep, talking and strategizing how their roles might change at Crossroads, as it became an equipping church where people were empowered to use their gifts.

"So how was your summer vacation?" Vernon asked Matt, sitting at Starbucks with his usual beverage. "You look tanned and rested."

"It was great. We had a wonderful time with the family in Colorado, just relaxing; a little hiking, fishing, and window-shopping. I was able to get in some good reading and thinking time as well. Not as much as I thought, but some."

"Good. I always take more than I ever get to. You'd think that after these many years I'd be a better judge of what I'll do, realistically. But we had fun, too. We visited our grandkids in Southern California, did Sea World, the San Diego Zoo, the beach. You know, the whole grandkid thing. Loved it."

"That's wonderful, Vernon. You look refreshed yourself."

"So are you ready to jump into the next step of this equipping process?"

"I am. What's next?"

"Well, we said there are three things that will hamstring a church from becoming an equipping church. One is a pastor who does not fully embrace or model it. The second is not having an equipping partner who'll champion this value throughout the other ministries. The third is a lack of structure that enables equipping, so that it never gets organized or becomes a part of the church culture."

"So does the pastor need to be the one who creates and runs the structure for equipping?"

"In general, no. But basically, the pastor is the social architect for a church, the cultural catalyst. For Crossroads to become an equipping church, you need to see the big picture so that you can help coach your partner and his or her team. You'll be more involved in the beginning, helping change church culture, and less involved as the church progresses; but you will want to be aware of what needs to happen for your church to succeed."

Vernon opened up his leather pad of paper and turned it lengthwise. He drew several lines and titles, then turned the pad toward Matt.

Building an Equipping Culture

Church Leadership   Ministry Leaders

Vernon pointed to "church leadership." "This involves the senior pastor, key staff, and influencers, as well as the governing board. You need to assess the current church culture. Most church cultures are not equipping in nature, so you'll want to look at a variety of things we often take for granted. For example, consider your history. I came to Westover not long after there'd been a bit of a scandal as to how the pastor was handling the finances. I never got the details, but by the time I got there, the council was pretty controlling, and you can see why. Earning trust was harder for me at first. Crossroads was a church plant, wasn't it?"

"Yes, I came a few years after it was started," Matt replied, stirring his coffee.

"OK, that will affect how they respond to a new idea in general, but especially one that changes how they think of you. Previous pastors are part of a church's culture. Passive or dominant pastors, hands-on or hands-off pastors, long tenures or scandalous ones, all of these create some expectations and precautions within a church."

"Hmm, that's interesting. I hadn't really taken that seriously."

"The demographics and traditions of the people are significant culture issues. If you have a group of church attendees from a certain worship tradition, or a split, or a certain socioeconomic demographic, that influences culture. For example, many years ago I pastored in a car factory town in Michigan. The unions ran that place. We had great people, but they'd respond a lot differently to equipping than people here. They were salt of the earth folk who took orders all day, so finding people comfortable leading a ministry at church wasn't easy.

"I have an African-American friend who pastors in the Dallas area. He said that in their tradition, when a man becomes a church leader, it's a place of high respect. For him to share that ministry or develop a team approach is far more challenging in that culture than others. So what are your sacred cows at Crossroad?"

"Sacred cows?"

"I mean those unwritten, seldom discussed assumptions that influence church culture. For example, Westover used to be even more traditional than it is now. We have certain expectations that, if you considered changing, people would think you were the Antichrist. For example, we celebrate communion weekly. Suggest something other and you might consider a job search. We used to have a giant pulpit. It took me five years to gradually replace that because it was a huge piece of furniture, dedicated by a wealthy, founding family, and was a part of a lot of our early pictures. People assumed if a sermon came from behind a smaller pulpit or, God-forbid, a music stand, then it wasn't blessed by God. That's a sacred cow."

"It's funny how when guys like me hear stories like that, we think we don't have any of those. But as you were talking, I realized we have our own sacred cows. They're just different. For example, if we tried to mess with the contemporary music and add some liturgy or a more meditative style, we'd probably hear about it."

"Good point. Even churches that think of themselves as very contemporary or edgy have their own cultural expectations. You find them when you start to mess with them. If you're not aware of them, you're more apt to be blindsided."

"So how does culture specifically affect what I'm trying to do now? Or is that a stupid question?"

"It's not obvious to most of us, and that's the point. Culture tends to be that invisible presence that makes your church unique to others. It's like spice in food, giving your church a distinct flavor from others. It's like cellophane wrap, sometimes invisible, but it keeps certain things in and other things out. When you try to move forward with a ministry idea and get pushback from people, assume it's a culture issue."

"What can you do about it, I mean, if you meet resistance?"

"Every church is different. That's why you can't simply import other ideas from other churches—which is what many pastors try to do after they read a book or attend a conference. Analyzing who you are as a church will help you design a plan that's most apt to be received. You want a sense of what you may be up against, in case you need to address that directly in your planning."

"All right," Matt said, taking notes on his laptop. "What kind of plan are we talking about?"

Vernon took a long sip from his latte, then continued. "Let's talk about the *who*, then the *what*. You'll want to gather an initial team. It could be key leaders from the board or your ministry areas, but I'd recommend it be an ad hoc team, made up of people who have influence but tend to be open to new ideas, and whom you think will embrace an equipping value. These are your strategists. You'll want a couple of people from your governance team, so they can communicate with their colleagues to avoid questions or trust concerns, but try to select the more progressive members."

"What do you call this team?" Matt asked.

"Oh, it doesn't matter. You can call it a dream team, or pastor's executive team, or just no name at all. At this point, I'd suggest keeping this more low-key and off the radar, so it doesn't draw much attention."

"Why is that? Sounds kind of sneaky, covert."

"New dreams are like babies. They tend to be very fragile. You need to care for a newborn with tenderness. The same is true of a new ministry idea. Surround it with people who are not threatened by new ideas, and let them read key books as a team, brainstorm, and begin to strategize a plan that will provide a churchwide reach. This might take 90 days. It might take a year. But do your homework. Don't just interrupt your previously scheduled program to bring them this breaking news. Launching a new idea is like starting a charcoal fire. You heap the coals together until it's white-hot, then you spread them around the grill. Bring your team together around this single theme, and only when it seems that you're committed to it as a team do you begin to include others in the process and expand the vision. As you begin to plan, you'll have a feel of how fast you should go."

"OK. So when do you roll it out?"

"I'd encourage you not to launch any sort of obvious initiative until you've taken some time to lay a biblical foundation with your ministry leaders. These are people, paid or unpaid, who oversee an area of ministry in the church. Take them through a multiweek discipleship series studying Exodus 18 and 19; Acts 6; Romans 12; 1 Corinthians 12; Ephesians 4; 1 Peter 2; and then perhaps one of the books we discussed, or a trip to an equipping church that includes a talk with the pastor and equipping ministry staff. Then you may want to top it off with a service project you do together outside the church. Don't underestimate the power of experiential learning: doing things together that involve physical activities and discussions."

Vernon continued. "You'll be amazed at how these kinds of activities will gel a team and add energy to your dream. But you're going to have to fan the flames at this point. You want to facilitate ownership in the equipping vision and wherever possible, affirm places where equipping is already going on in the church; you know, people who start doing it well. Lift up your good examples."

"Why so much behind-the-scenes work? It seems like a sermon series would be the typical way to do this."

"The reason is because you're most interested in helping build an equipping *culture*. Remember, this is not a program or a quick fix. It's something that will forever change your church both internally and externally—how it's known in the community. You want to do it right. Every church is different, so it will take a shorter time or more time based on where your ministry leaders are and how much biblical foundation is needed to help them understand it. It's your primary responsibility as pastor to make sure that church and ministry leaders understand why you're pursuing this value, and they also need to know that it's based on scriptural principles. The Bible is your greatest benefactor in avoiding resistance. Leaders are your strongest aid in making this a reality in your congregation."

"OK, I think I understand."

"I'm not saying you shouldn't preach on it during Sunday services. I'm merely saying that this should not be your very first step in the process. That would be more a matter of the vision casting, or perhaps the final message in a series including a vision cast."

"Vision's always a sort of mystical, fuzzy thing for me. I know everyone talks about it, but what do you mean by it?"

"I've got a great article on vision that I'll e-mail you. It will help you clarify your vision and, believe it or not, measure it. Vision is probably one of the most underestimated elements in a church, especially these days, because vision leaks. It gets lost in the deluge of messages, e-mails, and activities our people endure. Therefore, you have to keep emphasizing it over and over and in a variety of ways. People are so distracted and don't attend all the time, that you have to constantly re-vision, even if you feel like you're being redundant."

"Man, it's a lot of work, in addition to what you're already doing."

"It's pure physics."

Matt furrowed his brow. "What do you mean?"

"A body at rest tends to remain at rest. A body in motion…"

"…tends to remain in motion."

"Exactly. It takes a lot more energy to get this going in your church than it does to keep it going, but both require attention from leadership. You'll also want to make sure it's at all levels of the church and not the typical banner or snappy slogan. Create a multimedia presentation for people who are visually oriented. For those who learn best kinesthetically, have an activity involve their hands or sense of touch. And be sure that all the staff and ministry leaders are onboard with it as well, before you introduce it to the congregation. That's your best shot for making it a culture change, not just another fad or phase."

"Great, and thanks for sending me that article."

(For the free article on vision that Vernon referred to, go to www.rev.org, click on *Me to We* and then "Vision.")

Vernon turned his pad toward himself, and on the second line from the bottom, he wrote "Build Teams and Integrate Roles" above the line; below the line, three phrases: "Leadership Roles," "Equipping Ministry Team," and "Ministry Connectors." Then he turned it back to Matt.

Build Teams and Integrate Roles

Leadership Roles   Equipping Ministry Team   Ministry Connectors

Building an Equipping Culture

Church Leadership   Ministry Leaders

"At this level, your job as pastor is to help your governance board and ministry leaders begin functioning as teams. You start by clarifying senior leadership roles. Part of this has to do with how you as pastor are going to function, plus your staff and ministry leaders. Each team develops a sort of covenant, whether it is formal or informal, that holds each member accountable to the team. In other words, no more ministry alone."

"How would we do this?" Matt asked. "I mean there's so much going on already."

"I don't want to give you specifics because it will look different in your ministry context. But at Westover, we began to look at our weekly schedules during staff meetings. We actually listed the people we were getting together with for development and training purposes. Then, in a couple of sentences, what we were working on with these people. This did two things. It provided some accountability and also some creative ideas that helped us think how we might develop people around us. If a ministry leader didn't have anything specifically planned, then it stood out, and we made sure it became one of their goals. Whatever you do, don't assume it's happening, and don't say something like, 'OK, I hope all of you are developing your people' because most of them will nod their heads and just keep doing business as usual."

"I can see how that would happen. How many meetings have I been in where what we talked about never got implemented?"

"Probably a boatload. Leaving it up to everyone to do on their own just doesn't work very well, especially when you get started."

"So should there be someone in the director's position at this time?"

"Well, I'd get someone in that position as fast as possible because he or she will need to be developing the equipping team. That's not your job. Most important for you is to be sure you're helping the staff and board to begin functioning as a team. You'll at least want to make sure you've approved the position of an equipping director. You may have someone in mind by now, but this is where you'll clarify role expectations, lines of communication, accountability, and details such as any budget, initial training, office space, et cetera."

"I was wondering, because Chris said part of his job was to make sure you modeled equipping."

"That's right. *Every* member of *every* team needs to be accountable to each other, to make sure that team development and equipping are taking place within them. We call that a covenant. Your role is as a supporter and a facilitator, but you've got to empower each person with the authority to develop the team as he or she sees fit."

"I suppose since you're still working with leaders, it'd be good for me to be involved in more of a hands-on way."

"They need to see me—and you—modeling team and teaching the value, but we're not the hands-on person. Your director of equipping, or whatever you call the position, is the hands-on person. It's important for people to see you working on a team whose members respect each other. This builds trust and confidence."

"That makes sense."

"If people don't see this happening, then it's going to be hard for them to see much difference in how you're functioning as a pastor."

"Good point."

"You can help brainstorm with your new director. You can be a coach. But this person will need to figure out what gifts and roles are needed on the team, so that a variety of tasks can be accomplished. We're all tempted to be attracted to people who are like us, but good leaders will try to find people whose strengths make up for their weaknesses."

"Were you just winging it when you first began, or did God tell you what to do?"

"Well, while I was praying, a giant sheet descended from the sky, filled with all sorts of ministry descriptions and faces of people who made up our implementation teams," Vernon laughed. "Actually, it wasn't that far from the truth. We sent four of our people to some training that Sue and her staff put on periodically, offered by Church Volunteer Central. They came back with a boatload of ideas and some implementation strategies, which gave us a good head start. I think a church could figure it out on its own, but it's much better if you can learn from others. For example, you'll be able to avoid some of the mistakes we made because you're learning from someone who's a little further down the road."

"And I want you to know that Carmen and I appreciate that. We truly do."

"I know. I wasn't fishing for a compliment. I just think it's funny how often we try to figure things out by ourselves in the church, instead of sharing ideas, asking questions, or just watching how others do it."

Vernon pointed to "Ministry Connectors" with his pen. "We're going to come back to this in a few minutes."

Vernon turned the sheet with the matrix back to himself. On the second line from the top, he wrote "Build Support Systems" just above the line; and below it, three phrases: "Administrative Support," "Strategic Support," and "Prayer Support." He turned the pad toward Matt.

"At this point, your role as pastor is to be the advocate and to champion this value from the pulpit and among key leaders, as needed. It's good for you to have an understanding of what needs to happen, but that's pretty much it."

	Build Support Systems	
Administrative Support	Strategic Support	Prayer Support
	Build Teams and Integrate Roles	
Leadership Roles	Equipping Ministry Team	Ministry Connectors
	Building an Equipping Culture	
Church Leadership		Ministry Leaders

Vernon pointed to the words to the right on the second line and continued. "One thing you can help advocate is making sure 'prayer support' happens at a variety of levels. Now that I think of it, I hope I haven't come across as too cerebral about this whole thing. Obviously, you know my heart, how I believe this approach to pastoring is founded on Scripture. But you can't just 'do it' like Nike says. Your staff and ministry leaders really should be seeking God's wisdom, not to mention the power and peace of the Spirit. Your equipping team needs that same kind of prayer support as they wrestle with things like ministry descriptions, assessments, and systems."

"I don't think I ever got the idea from you that this was just a human process," Matt said. "But I am glad you reminded me to make that a priority. Sometimes I think we pastors get so caught up in all the church growth and ministry practices that we forget to go back to the basics."

"Yeah, in this case, the basics really aren't basic, are they? They're what power all this other stuff we do so that it makes sense and works the way God wants. So don't assume prayer is taking place. Make it a concerted effort, in part so people don't think you're just falling for some new-fangled way to involve more people or avoid doing your job. This *is* your job!"

"I like that."

"All right, let's look here on the left. 'Administrative support' is more of the tactical things your equipping team is going to need to create. We mentioned them in the past, but here's where their team helps create the ministry descriptions. Once you've created ministry descriptions, you'll want to start tracking people, like following up on them after a new members' class or spiritual gifts seminar. The team needs to figure out how they'll keep in touch with people newly assigned to a ministry, making sure they feel comfortable and cared for and are receiving training. And you'll want to know when people leave a ministry."

"That seems like a lot of details. How in the world do you come up with all these things?"

"You don't; your equipping team does it. When your business is people, you'd better not let them fall through the cracks. One of my greatest frustrations is when ministry leaders invite people to consider their ministries, and then they drop the ball or have pitiful follow through."

"Yeah, it's easy to do."

"But whether it's easy or hard, it doesn't matter. What does matter is how we treat people. By creating and integrating systems, we're more apt to do what Jesus did—love people. These tracking systems are just tools. It's people who matter."

"Can you recommend any software or systems?"

"Ugh, you got me there. To be honest, I'm not in that area, and I don't know what we use. Someone was telling me about software that CVC recommended called Buzz Central. It's designed to integrate the various ministry components and communicate easily, but you'd have to talk to Chris about that. Better yet, have your director of equipping talk to Chris. You'll want to empower your team to implement it. Have the equipping team administrator put together a task force to research the best software for your church culture and what it is you want to capture. Just make sure you don't have someone make up your own system, who could end up leaving with the code and is the only one who knows how to use it. Then you're really sunk."

"Oh yeah. We've done that before. So what does 'strategic support' mean?"

"Primarily it's just more of what your equipping team will need to create with the admin support. You know, space, facilities…"

"And money," Matt interrupted.

"Yes, budget. And of course you'll wind up with some guidelines so that everyone is clear about what is needed, how things are prioritized, accountability, and who is empowered to do what. As this ministry gets developed, you'll need to be an advocate. Make sure they have freedom and influence to do their job. When you do, your life gets easier."

"You're saying it's a good investment."

"Everything's about stewardship, when you think about it. We've gotten to the point now where we have designated office space, computers, copiers, phones, and supplies for people who are unpaid but fill various ministry roles. They even have keys to those offices so they can work when they like. And this is not the used, leftover stuff, tucked away next to the janitor's closet. To be honest, it's as nice or nicer than the equipment in the rest of the offices. Several people have passwords so they can access records and files over the Internet at home or when they travel. I may have mentioned earlier that we even have some paid staff who report to unpaid ministry leaders. All of this lets people know that we take their ministry seriously."

"Was it difficult getting to that point? I can't imagine this happening at Crossroads, at least not for a long time, even though it makes sense."

"Patience, patience. You have to start where you're at. It's taken us years, but there comes a point when you reach critical mass, and it sort of kicks into a higher level. Jim Collins, in *Good to Great*, called it the *flywheel principle*, where you keep doing the right thing over and over, and suddenly the momentum builds. That's when you know it's become a part of your church culture. What also helps is if some of your key businesspeople catch this vision. When people find out that instead of hiring a dozen paid professionals you can hire six, plus support staff—and have a good chunk of money left over for programs—they'll start to get excited."

"So it sounds like I'm working myself out of a job."

"Oh no, on the contrary! When your leaders see you tapping the potential of the church, you'll be in far more demand than ever. No one's going to let go of a pastor who works that way. You'll be writing your ticket to job security. Plus, you'll be having the time of your life. I can't believe they pay me to do my job. But…"

"I know, I know, there was a price to pay."

"That was our second lesson, wasn't it? Good job."

ernon turned the paper pad back toward himself. On the left side of the top line, he wrote "Prepare" above the line, and below it he wrote "Assimilation" and "Biblical Foundations."

"This line has to do with how people in your congregation experience equipping in your church. In this section, you're basically answering two questions: 'How do I understand and become part of the church?' and 'What is the biblical basis for service?' By the latter, we're referring to the priesthood of the believers, about leadership, gifts, responding to the call of God, as well as giving and receiving care."

Prepare		
Assimilation Biblical Foundations		
Build Support Systems		
Administrative Support	Strategic Support	Prayer Support
Build Teams and Integrate Roles		
Leadership Roles	Equipping Ministry Team	Ministry Connectors
Building an Equipping Culture		
Church Leadership	Ministry Leaders	

Matt took notes. "So this is where the rubber meets the road?"

"This is where it happens. This is about the assimilation process and laying the biblical foundations with people so they can see that what you're doing is about their spiritual growth, not just a nifty program to recruit more workers. I guess I can't emphasize this enough. I'm convinced that the primary reason we don't see more spiritual growth is that people are not serving in the areas of their gifts, and people are not receiving ministry from others in the areas of their gifts. When this happens, God's grace is thwarted; and when that happens, people don't mature in their faith. This is really all about discipleship."

"That really does make so much sense when you put it in that context."

"I've seen it with my own eyes. We're missing it, big time, in our churches. Only God can transform lives, and when we put people without God-given gifts in areas where they're expected to serve, lives aren't transformed. It's just that simple. How long will it take us to figure that out?"

"Talk to me about assimilation, because we're forever trying to close the back door. Sometimes I feel more like the chaplain of a slow-moving parade than a pastor."

"Well, we've been able to change the revolving doors on our church to normal ones, but you're never going to be able to lock them—and you wouldn't want to. The great thing about serving is that if it's done well, you're going to eventually have a lot of visitors streaming through your front doors. The reason is that when you begin recognizing and ordaining people to use their gifts in the community, people will see their 'good deeds and praise your Father in heaven.' That's in Matthew 5:16."

"I like the way that sounds. Outreach seems like it's getting tougher and tougher all the time."

"People today want to see *action* before they want to hear us talk about *faith*. It's never been more important for people to put up or shut up."

"So how do you assimilate newcomers?"

"You'll have to figure that out yourself. To be honest, I don't think there's any one right way. We've tried a bunch of things at Westover. We used to have those registration pads that get passed down the rows on Sunday morning. Then we offered gifts for newcomers if they stood up, or later, when they turned in a card at the visitor center. Now, we use a variety of ways, but mostly encouraging them to sign a card. We get contact info when they sign their child into our nursery or children's programs. Sometimes it's not until our visitors' or membership classes. It's not easy."

"I was wondering if I was missing some secret formula."

"The point is finding something that works for you and sticking to it. You can't stop. You can't let down. Do whatever it takes to help people find friendships. I read a study put together by the Gallup organization that said people who feel like they have friends at church are more involved and feel like they're growing spiritually, more than those who do not."

Vernon continued. "Another thing that we've found, and I know it sounds funny, but we make sure that as much as possible, there's some sort of food or refreshment included in our meetings and events. Sometimes it's just that moment you stop to grab a snack or cup of coffee that you pause to meet someone. There's something nurturing and bonding that takes place when people share food together…"

"Yeah, and join Weight Watchers together."

"I know, you don't have to overdo it or have junk food. But I think there's a reason why the early church ate together in people's homes like in Acts 2."

"So how do you teach these principles of serving and gifting?"

"We do it on Sunday mornings a couple of times a year. But Chris and his team have a pretty strong teaching program that lays the biblical foundations for spiritual growth, maturity, gifts, and the priesthood of believers. We also have small-group Bible studies and—believe it or not—we teach it in our elementary and youth group ministries as well."

"Really?"

"Why not? The best time to teach kids about serving and helping others with your gifts is before their moral cement has set, most say, by the age of 14. If you want to grow great Christians, you'd better get them early. We help our age-group ministry leaders use kids and youth in ministry roles. That way, by the time they become adults, they're already familiar with their responsibility."

"I love that! We could do that."

"The cool thing is that when the kids come home after doing a serving project, or we present a video clip during the worship service showing youth working on an elderly person's home, it gets to the adults. We've also started providing family projects, where all ages come together and experience serving together. The power of these single events is that it whets the appetite for other serving, plus it bonds people in the process. Actually, that's helped our membership process because when people see what we're doing and connect with a few other people, they think, *Hey, I like this church. I think I'd like to join.*"

"Hmm, that's interesting. Sometimes I think we try to get people to join, and then get them in a ministry."

"I think it tends to work the other way. It's just that if you require a certain teaching process for membership, at least you're more confident that the people joining the church really do understand the biblical basics underlying your values. The bottom line is that you want to help create a culture of serving and connecting. Preach it and teach it wherever you can. Work within the areas already functioning in your church to welcome people into service."

*Connecting
People*

Vernon took the paper; on the center of the top line he wrote "Connect" above the line, and below it he wrote "Discovery" as well as "Matching and Placement."

"So you start with Scriptures, laying a foundation, and then you have to get to the very practical aspects of serving. 'Connect' strives to answer two different questions for everyone in the church: 'Who am I and what are my needs?' and 'What ministry opportunities best fit my gifts and interests?'"

Prepare	Connect	
Assimilation	Discovery	
Biblical	Matching	
Foundations	& Placement	
	Build Support Systems	
Administrative Support	Strategic Support	Prayer Support
	Build Teams and Integrate Roles	
Leadership Roles	Equipping Ministry Team	Ministry Connectors
	Building an Equipping Culture	
Church Leadership	Ministry Leaders	

"Sounds like a pretty tall order to fill," Matt said. "You try to take these on in your workshop?"

"Well, hopefully we begin doing this before they attend the workshop."

"What do you mean?"

"What I mean is that we want people to feel like they're loved and cared for in our church, that their needs are important to us, and if possible, being met. If people don't experience practical ways in which their needs are being met, then it's going to be hard to sell it in a workshop. When people discover how God has made them in the context of receiving ministry from others, they're far more apt to get involved themselves."

"That really makes sense. So when they get to the workshop, how do you teach this?"

"We don't get heavy and philosophical. We try to make it very practical and user-friendly. But when you think about it, if you tap this innate human desire, you're going to find a lot of motivation. I know there are a lot of reasons Rick Warren's *Purpose-Driven Life* took off the way it did, but people really are interested in discovering their divine purpose, beyond paying a mortgage and planning their next vacation."

"So how do you do this?"

"I think that the answer is not so much a *what* but a *how*. In other words, don't get stuck on one of these plug-and-play gift assessments. There are several good ones out there. 'Network,' 'S.H.A.P.E.,' and Church Volunteer Central have ones they make available free to their members. In fact, I think you can even put it on your Web site if you want. But if possible, I'd recommend that you help people discover their gifts in a context of other people—and through Scripture, of course. This is a very exciting process. Plus, a lot of churches never capture this information. I think that's a bad stewardship decision. Human nature being what it is, we're all prone to procrastination and letting life crowd out these new discoveries."

"So what does this look like for you guys?"

"Well, we start by finding out how we can do a better job caring for people. People are so private and self-sufficient these days that we explore how we can serve them better in the context of caring for others. Sometimes we learn very helpful things."

"Interesting. I'd never think of that."

"Then we help them discover their gifts through Scripture, by looking at Ephesians 4 and the other gifts passages. We connect this with personal calling and try to uncover their passions. And we top it off with a brief personality assessment. Then we discuss taking next steps. That's a helicopter view of what we try to accomplish in this training."

"So are you involved in any of this?"

"I used to do part of it, along with the equipping director. But now I only do a little of the teaching in our membership class. I'll usually drop in for a few minutes to affirm 'I believe this,' but it seems to have more credibility if lay leaders are running it. I do mention it in our newcomers' social. I think it's crucial for the pastor to teach the entire church what he or she thinks is fundamental. But I delegate the implementation to others."

Vernon paused, then continued. "Discovery needs to be holistic. It's about helping people understand their gifts, experiences, passions, skills, talents, and also what their needs are. If you just teach gifts, you give people the impression that they're filling ministry slots, and that doesn't motivate many people."

"That's good. Do you require people to be involved in a ministry when they become members?"

"We don't, but we highly encourage it. We teach that being an official member involves committing your time, talent, and treasure to this local body of believers."

"Does that scare people away?"

"About 80 percent cross the line. By doing that, we set the standards high. In fact, when we introduce people to the congregation as they become members, we mention their gifts and area of ministry involvement so people can know what they're bringing to the congregation. To be honest, most of the time people get involved in ministry before they join our church. For us, it's been a way that people get connected in relationships. But if they don't, we try to make membership class an opportunity to discover and experience serving."

"That's a great idea. I think we've been making membership too easy, like we're just so happy that you've joined us, we're not worried about what you bring to the game."

"Good point! Let me add one more thing to the discovery process. I think this has been key for us. If at all possible, make sure your equipping team establishes a way to provide a personal interview. A good face-to-face or phone interview can uncover more than an assessment. Plus it's a way to personalize the experience, and it significantly raises the chances of making a good ministry connection. This can take place anywhere, at any time, but the time that's worked for us is right after the newcomers' class."

"What goes on in the interview?"

"Well, I'm using the term 'interview' with you, but we don't use it in our ministry because it can sound kind of scary or intimidating. We say something like, 'I just want to meet you,' or 'We'd like to get to know you better,' or 'Let's just have cup a of coffee after church.' We like to refer to it as a conversation for holistic discovery—sort of like neighbors chatting over the picket fence—to get to know someone and discover where he or she may need ministry or be ready to minister."

"That sounds more inviting."

"It doesn't need to be long, anywhere from half an hour to an hour and a half, usually. You can talk to Chris about this, but again, you don't have to be the one who figures out the details. Just make sure it's a part of the discovery process. Gifts are one thing, but passions and stories are another. When you watch someone describe a time in their life where they felt fulfilled doing a task or ministry, you can see their eyes light up. A paper or online assessment doesn't capture all this info."

"Wow, great idea. A lot of work, but a great idea."

"Obviously, your equipping team will want a way to capture this info. Don't just send it home with people or let the equipping staff work from memory. That's a part of the system we discussed, which includes filing a written recap, and follow-up. The system doesn't have to be technical. It's a way to ensure records are kept and that follow-up does indeed happen. But that's not your job. Your job is to cast vision, to be an advocate, and make sure the equipping team has the resources needed to do their work."

Vernon continued, "The key is to care for people with the process, not just after it. No one wants to feel like a commodity or just another warm body in a cattle call for volunteers. They want to matter."

"Yeah, I've felt like a cowboy from time to time."

"And probably your congregation members felt like they were a herd, but not being heard. This is about a customized approach to making a good ministry connection. You can't mass-produce disciples. Jesus didn't try, so why should we? But you can see that if you want to provide an individualized journey, you need a lot of help."

"So what do you do with all this great information after you capture it?"

"That's when *matching and placement* come into play," Vernon said, pointing to these words on the paper. "Once people experience the results of an effective discovery process, they need to know the *how* and *what* of their next steps. For example, if someone finds out they have the gift of hospitality, how does the church take this knowledge and create a good ministry match for the person? We should not leave it up to them. The church must assume leadership in making the process of connection effective. There are various ways to ensure this matching and placement occurs. Once someone completes an interview or a discovery-process information sheet, then the connection can be solidified as the info is communicated to a particular area that fits the bill. Another way is to show them the possibilities. We have notebooks full of ministry descriptions categorized by gifts, interests, and skills. Recently, we put these online so that people can search for ministry opportunities inside and outside the church."

Matt dramatically stopped his note-taking and looked up as if in shock. "That is *so* cool."

Vernon laughed. "Yeah, we had a computer programmer who saw our three-ring binders and said, 'We can put this online and make it a lot easier and faster.' So we turned him loose. Anyway, you don't start there; but there should be a place where people can learn what is available. That also requires our ministry leaders to do their job in terms of defining various ministry roles, breaking it down into tasks, time, and talents."

"Wow, what a great process. Very cool."

"It doesn't stop there."

"There's more?"

"**Y**ou want to make sure a person experiences the discovery process, and you want to learn how you can serve this person," Vernon said. "But you also want to make sure this person has a great first experience in a ministry, or at least see if it's a good fit. That's the role of the Ministry Connectors."

"The what?" Matt asked.

"Ministry Connectors. Remember that part of the chart we skipped a few minutes ago?" Vernon took his pen and tapped the paper on the end of the second line. "Most churches are so thankful to have another warm body that they do nothing to see if there's a good fit. Plus, people want to make friends, not just give their time and talent. Relationships are the glue that keeps people together even when it becomes inconvenient to serve. Most ministry leaders are consumed with the task, so that no matter how well-intended they are, they can't give the attention needed to a new person. So the role of the Ministry Connector is to follow up and connect, to ensure orientation is available, to make sure the candidate gets a ministry description, and to make sure that training, consistent affirmation, feedback, and evaluation occur within the ministry area."

"So how does this work?"

	youth connector	children connector	worship connector	hospitality connector	admin. connector
equipping					
outreach					
leadership development					

"Remember the matrix I showed you several weeks ago?"

"Yes, in fact," Matt paused as he pulled out a file folder from the pocket in his computer bag, and leafed through several of the graphs that Vernon had drawn for him. "Here it is," Matt said, sliding the lined piece of paper in front of Vernon.

Vernon looked at the sheet. "Yep, that's it." He took his pen and wrote the word "connector" under each name on top of the vertical columns: "youth," "children," "worship," "hospitality," and "admin."

"You want to make sure that your ministry leader embraces and practices the equipping value. Just as I have a partner in Chris, each ministry leader should have a partner who focuses on this one key task in their area of ministry. That's a Ministry Connector."

"So help me better understand why we need this. It's starting to look like levels of a bureaucracy."

"We've found that sometimes leaders aren't as thorough in matching people with the best roles in a ministry team, or they revert to old habits. Ministry Connectors help make sure the various systems that the equipping team develop for the church are utilized in the various ministries."

"So are these Ministry Connectors a part of the equipping team or the specific ministry team?"

"Ideally they'd be a part of both, at least when you're smaller and getting started. You want to find someone passionate about the specific ministry, but who also understands the equipping value and is in touch with the equipping director."

"So let me get this straight. You have a person in each ministry area, like children and youth and worship and the like, who is *not* the leader, but who interviews and meets with someone interested in the ministry area."

"That's right."

"That sounds kind of risky. It seems like a person joining a ministry would want to talk to the leader directly, and the leader would want to make sure he or she's getting the person needed on the team. I'm not sure if our ministry leaders would want to have someone else picking ministry team members."

"That's why the ministry leader and the connector need to work together, just as I do with the director of equipping ministry. I have to trust that person. If it is a key role on the team, then include the leader. But the connector provides the follow-up, and at times, can serve as a buffer because people on the team have a relationship with the Ministry Connector. This improves communication, and the connector can run interference for the ministry leader."

"What if the ministry leader meets someone after church who would be a great fit for the team? Does he still go through the connector?"

"When this is working well, the leader might say, 'Could you talk to our Ministry Connector? Her contact info is…' or 'Could I have our Ministry Connector contact you?' The key here is communication and inclusion, because otherwise, even a good leader may drop the ball, fail to provide proper orientation, or get preoccupied with all the other things he or she is doing to lead the team. Because of the Ministry Connector's key role, it's important for this person to be on the ministry leadership team."

"That is interesting. I'd never have thought of that. I can't imagine that being easy to sell to your ministry leaders, at least initially."

"That was one of our challenges. In fact, that was one of those times when Chris came to me and said, 'I need you to talk to the staff.'"

"So how did it go?"

"Well, I talked to them, and together we helped our ministry leaders see this was a win-win for everyone involved. Most bought in, but some were hesitant. I had to communicate that participation was not optional. This was going to be our new normal and everyone would do it. The staff heard what I was saying, if you know what I mean."

"So you pulled executive rank?"

"I guess you could say something like that. Fortunately, it proved to be the right call. When the ministry leaders began developing and working with their Ministry Connectors, it lightened their loads and allowed them to focus on what they loved— doing ministry. And it added more people in the right positions, because they were assimilated properly."

Vernon continued, "Plus, this person helps promote the values of equipping that our church embraces. Ministries tend to do their own thing, have their own system, and often do not communicate well with other ministries. An equipping goal is to integrate the ministries so you improve communication, track people better, and avoid letting them fall through the cracks. The connector becomes a liaison with the equipping ministry as a whole. When you get started, this person receives ongoing training from the director of equipping ministry; makes sure the new team member info is in the database files; gathers personal info such as birth date and family member's names; and also lets the equipping ministry know if the person leaves a ministry and that proper follow-up took place. As you grow, you'll have a single person on the core equipping team who coordinates with the various Ministry Connectors."

"Wow, I can see how that would help people from getting lost, especially as a church grows."

"We teach our leaders that people are like eggs. When you drop them, there's usually a mess to clean up."

"Too true."

"The power of this role is that it helps keep the equipping value and system present throughout all the ministries. It lightens the load of leaders, while at the same time, helps improve the quality of the experience for the team member. Plus, it's a valuable way to involve people in ministry. After all, the church is here to serve people. This is an important way we do it."

"Now that you explain it, the Ministry Connector seems like a pretty important role."

"Definitely! These are the ligaments that hold the body together, mentioned in Ephesians 4. It's one of those key points that gets overlooked unless you develop a churchwide system that integrates ministries. I can't emphasize how important these team members are in terms of constantly communicating and keeping track of ministry-team staffing. The more people you involve in service, the more challenging it becomes to communicate clearly. Therefore, you need more people whose responsibility it is to do this."

"Man, I'm glad you're helping us."

Vernon took the paper with the four lines. On the right side of the top line, he wrote "Equip" above it, and below it he wrote "Growth" and "Recognition and Reflection."

"How are you doing on time? We're almost done with this plan for implementing equipping in a local church."

Matt looked at his watch. "Hey, I've got all the time it takes. I feel bad for you."

Prepare	Connect	Equip
Assimilation Biblical Foundations	Discovery Matching & Placement	Growth Recognition & Reflection
	Build Support Systems	
Administrative Support	Strategic Support	Prayer Support
	Build Teams and Integrate Roles	
Leadership Roles	Equipping Ministry Team	Ministry Connectors
	Building an Equipping Culture	
Church Leadership		Ministry Leaders

"Oh I'm fine. As long as this is helpful, I'm game. OK, let's look at *equipping*. This word may not be the best way to describe this, because the whole thing is really about equipping. I think they originally used this term in the graphic because it describes what may be the most unique about a church that really 'gets' the Ephesians 4 value." Vernon tapped the upper right-hand corner of the paper with his pen. "We're going to answer the questions 'How do I get ongoing training in ministry?' and 'How do I sustain my ministry and grow spiritually?'"

"Let me get that down. So what makes these questions so important, or at least so different, from what most churches do?"

"Well, as we've noted, a majority of churches don't do any serious teaching or training in the area of spiritual gifts and service. They're fine to let the pastor run the show and add some token time here and there whenever a plea for more help shows up in the bulletin or during the Sunday announcements. But even among the churches that occasionally teach gifts and assessment, very few of these ever get to *equipping*. In my opinion, leadership training is the single most important element, because if everyone knows their gifts but you haven't identified and trained leaders, you're sunk."

"So what takes place in this section of the plan you're describing?"

"This section separates the adults from the kids—those serious about equipping and the wanna-bes. The goal at this point is to help people grow as they serve. I wish I had some cute acrostic for this, but here are the components of the growth process. The first is *training*. It may be as simple as a thorough orientation, or there may be essential skills that need to be taught. For example, in our small-group ministry, we require an initial half-day training for potential leaders. Then we assign them to existing, proven leaders for a period of 90 days, to let them see how a good small group functions. Then we have them try leading for a few sessions. If everything looks good, the mentor signs off on the person and the small-group leader is free to develop his or her own group. If more training is suggested, then we'll figure out how to do that before releasing the small-group leader to be in charge of his or her own group."

"Can you give me an example of the training a small-group leader might go through?"

"You mean, how do you facilitate a group? If you're like most untrained small-group leaders, you think this is your little congregation to preach at. The other day, I saw a small group meeting in a coffee shop. There was a leader and his wife with about eight college students, sitting around tables. Did that guy understand the skill of catalyzing conversation among others? No. It was a one-man show—he just lectured them. So we make sure our small-group leaders know the fine art of asking strategic questions. We even measure the talk time, making sure they know what it feels like to talk less than 25 percent of the time. We show them how to analyze body language when group members are feeling bored, or angry, or shut down. It's pretty impressive."

"Vernon, this sounds incredible, really, but there's no way we could pull this off. That's a lot of time and commitment."

"In time, my friend, in time. Don't compare where we are with where you are. We've been at it for a long time. Baby steps. That's what you need. Look at the graph; it's near the end of the development process. Hang in there."

"I see the importance, I really do. I guess I'm just a bit overwhelmed with all that goes into it."

"So was Moses when Jethro suggested he raise a team to serve Israel, but over time, it happened. That's why this next principle is important—*affirmation*. It's the *One Minute Manager* all over. Catch people doing something right. Affirm a person's commitment, skill, attitude, or effort. Be as specific as possible. Affirmation can be a tool for growth. We even have a training session for our leaders, making sure they know how to do it well and in a variety of ways."

"So to affirm implies that you have someone who is watching."

"Exactly. You can't just assume this is happening naturally. The reason this is important is because the next step is *feedback*. You want to let the new ministry team member know how he or she is doing. Start with the positives first—the affirmations—and then lovingly make a suggestion or two to help make the person's ministry even more effective."

"You do this with volunteers?"

"Well, 'we' do, meaning that all the ministry leaders are trained to do this and are responsible to provide feedback. But why not?"

"Because they're giving their time. They're donating their talent. Seems like you'd offend people and they'd quit."

"The key is in how you do it. That's a training piece for ministry leaders and connectors. When this becomes a part of your culture, feedback gathering and evaluation are expected. We've set the bar so low in most churches that it's no wonder people bring their leftovers to ministry. 'Oh it doesn't matter how bad you sing or how little effort you put into your Sunday school lesson or if you show up late as an usher; God loves you and so do we.' That's garbage!" Vernon pounded the table with his fist. Some people turned around to look. "Show me one place in the Bible where God is satisfied with mediocrity."

"I can't," Matt said. "But reality says that we can't expect that much from our volunteers."

"I disagree. We get what we expect, and if we expect people to give us their shoddy leftovers, then that's what we'll receive. You reap what you sow."

"Man, you really believe this, don't you?"

"I believe it because I see it every week. We've got people who make their ministry the best part of their week because they realize we believe in them. We raise the bar. But you do it slowly, progressively, a little at a time."

"So how do you generate this feedback?"

"Evaluation. We evaluate what we do. We perform post-mortems on our events and take the time to analyze what went well, what didn't, what others experienced, and what we can do better next time. We do this on personal and team levels. The key is doing it in love, making sure grace prevails; but grace minus excellence makes grace cheap and meaningless."

"Good theology. I'm not sure how we miss that so often in ministry."

"Part of it has to do with the last ingredient. The key is *ongoing leader development*. If there's one place you don't want to scrimp, that is in growing your leaders. Your ministry leaders are the ones who'll be making sure that training, affirmation, feedback, and evaluation is happening in their area of ministry. They may not be doing it themselves, but they'll make sure it's happening because they want to succeed, whether they're paid or unpaid. And don't just consider ministry inside the church. One way the local church has failed in the past is inviting people to serve and then quickly moving on, thinking we've done our job, without providing any substantial training. We need to set them up to succeed."

(For a free color download of Church Volunteer Central's Equipping Church graphic, go to www.ChurchVolunteerCentral.com, click on "Pastors" and then "Equipping Church Plan.")

"What do you mean, 'We need to set them up to succeed'?" Matt asked.

"I mean you've probably already got a lot of people in your congregation who are using their gifts but aren't being affirmed or trained as ministers," Vernon said. "For example, do you have anyone in your church who's coaching kids' baseball, soccer, football, basketball, or T-ball?"

"Sure, several."

"So why not affirm them for their ministry to kids?"

"Well, I guess because it's not in our church."

"Why not give them a little extra training, pray for them, and commission them as extensions of your church? Chances are they're extending God's grace to these kids and their families. May as well raise their vision and maybe even give them some ideas for viewing what they do as more of a ministry. We found out that the baseball coach at the community college was a Christian, so we invited him to come do a Saturday morning clinic for the parents in our church who were T-ball and Little League coaches. We also had a counselor provide some tips in working with kids and identifying symptoms of family problems. Then we commissioned the coaches with some prayer and dedication. You'd be amazed at how well they responded to this. And because we planted that seed, people started viewing their coaching positions as a ministry. A few new families even came as a result of those coaches."

"I never thought of that. What are some other areas like this?"

"Well, we don't do it—I'm not sure why—but I heard of a church that 'ordains' their stay-at-home moms of infants and toddlers, who may not have time to do anything around the church or community because of their stage of life, but they're building the kingdom. Why not affirm them?"

"Hmm, that's interesting."

"Unless you've surveyed or asked your people, chances are you're unaware of a lot of serving roles going on, such as hospice, the Red Cross, Meals On Wheels, tutoring after school, Habitat for Humanity, or any number of service projects that corporations are now hosting for their employees. We're regularly monitoring how many of our people are involved in community services, and we're recognizing them publicly."

"But doesn't that take away from people serving inside your church?"

"Well, if you're not intentional, chances are you will forever be looking for more people; but even when you take equipping seriously, you'll probably only be able to involve about 50 percent of your people inside the walls of your church. Then you'll be saturated."

"Run that by me again?"

"The typical church only has ministry opportunities for about half of its people. Don't get me wrong. We don't always have people waiting in line for some of our roles. Sometimes we have to wrestle with staff who lose people to outreach-type ministries, but when your primary goal is to grow people, you don't care where they're serving— as long as it's the right place for them. You're more concerned with helping them find a place of meaningful service than you are with staffing your children's ministry or finding janitors."

"That is revolutionary. So you actually facilitate this? You help people plug in to community service as a type of ministry."

"We do. Plus, we're involved with helping train them as well. Our goal is to help them learn skills they can use at work, in their neighborhood, and as a means of reaching out to others. Imagine what it would be like if people started thinking of church as a place to go to get life skills. That's our dream: to provide English as second language classes, marriage and parenting seminars, money management, résumé writing and interviewing skills—other topics like these."

"I've never thought about how far you could take all this. I guess when you're only thinking about filling slots, you look at it one way, but when you're investing in a process for spiritual growth, you see things a lot differently."

"That you do. We want people to feel fulfilled in ministry and life. It's a holistic approach, not just a serve-the-church thing. The church has so much to offer people. It's about discovering their unique niche in life, how God wants to use them. John Ed Mathison, the pastor of a big equipping church in the South, told me that they call their equipping ministry niche picking. He says, 'When they pick their niche, they're a lot less likely to nitpick.'"

The two men laughed. "That sounds good to me," Matt said.

"There's a whole new movement happening in churches across the country. Some refer to it as the externally focused churches. My friend, Rick Rusaw, wrote a book called *The Externally Focused Church*. He said that their church used to draw large crowds of people to their events, but he eventually asked the question, 'What good is it doing?' They decided to stop these big events and focus on impacting their community. For example, every month, Rick brings together a small group of community leaders—a few sharp business professionals, the chief of police, and other strategic thinkers—and facilitates a meeting where they brainstorm solutions to city problems. These aren't people from their church for the most part, but they meet at the church and wrestle with social problems and plan solutions."

Vernon continued, "Over the years, Rick's church has become a dominant influence in their city, so that even school officials, city leaders, and a lot of nonprofits come to them for advice, support, and resources. He says you have to earn the right to be heard. Most of us in the church want to be heard without earning that right, which is why our communities don't listen to us for the most part. There are a lot of churches like them now, who are showing their communities what faith with skin looks like."

"That is what we'd love to do. It just seems like it takes so much energy, just to keep your own programs going, let alone think of getting into the community."

"You'd find that most externally focused congregations teach equipping because it does take a critical mass of resources to just maintain a church. But after you get your basics covered, you can overflow into the neighborhoods. That's when people start noticing your church, and as a result, visitors start coming because they've interacted with your people out in the community."

"Let your deeds shine, so they can honor your Father."

"Amen!"

(For a free downloadable article, "The Externally Focused Church," go to www.rev.org, click on Me to We, and then Externally Focused.)

Next Steps

"**A**ll right, now you've gotten an overview of the big picture," Vernon said, handing the hand-drawn graph to Matt.

"It's a little overwhelming," Matt said, staring at the sheet.

"That's the beauty of this. It's not up to you to figure out how to do it. You're an empowerer, not an emperor. You want some next step ideas for getting started?"

"I'd love them."

"OK, you've already discovered this, that the tyranny of the urgent is your biggest enemy. You'll be very tempted to continue doing business as usual, instead of finding time to work on this behind the scenes. Every week, when you plan your agenda, make sure you carve out time for developing people, connecting with potential leaders, and working with your equipping partner. You'll have to say no to some great things and give up immediate gratification for long-term benefit, but don't let up."

"I can see that's going to be a challenge already."

"I also found that momentum can be deceiving. I thought that if I preached a few sermons, got people to take spiritual gifts surveys, and promoted a ministry fair, that's all it would take. Momentum is like the gas tank in a car. The gauge is always moving toward empty and requires frequent refilling."

"That's so true."

Vernon opened his leather folder and pulled out some notes. "I jotted down some ideas as I was thinking about this the other day. Another initial mistake we made was to measure the wrong things. At first we only looked at how many people were signed up for a ministry. But later we discovered that many people weren't really in the right places. Sometimes you realize that you have to move people around, let them experiment, and let them back down. The goal is a right fit, not just any fit. Don't just measure how many are involved, but try to estimate how right the fit is and how satisfied the people are in their role of service."

Vernon looked down his list and continued. "Here are some roadblocks we ran into. A while back we talked about staff, but it's not just selling them on the basic concept, it's also continuing to hold them accountable. When you have some laypeople drop the ball or let a ministry leader down, it's tempting for staff to say, 'See, I knew this was a bad idea; volunteers aren't dependable.' Then they revert back to doing it themselves.

"For example," Vernon explained, "one of our part-time staff members, who was a pastor, used to facilitate a few recovery groups that met at our church. He'd come and open the doors and just be available. We encouraged him to develop a team of people to help him do this so it didn't ride on his shoulders. He found a man with a heart for it. One night, he got a call from the AA leader who said they were outside the church and the man hadn't shown up to unlock the doors. Our staff member was in the middle of a family event, left, and came down to let in the group. He was so frustrated with that volunteer that he called the man and told him he wasn't needed anymore. Then the staff member wound up doing it himself again, because he felt like he couldn't depend on someone if he wasn't paid. We had to sit down with this pastor and talk to him about training, and second chances, and to keep trying."

Vernon continued, "Another roadblock is a lack of planning. It really does take more effort initially to organize everyone, set up communication links, workshops, expand the database, and cast the vision. I'd really make sure that you and your partner, and eventually his or her team, work on a plan to cover these areas. Oh, here's another one."

"Wow, sounds slow going," Matt said.

"Well, I think that one of the biggest challenges of roadblocks is when you're unaware of them. You'll be much better off if you see and prepare for them as much as possible. I've never figured this one out fully. No matter how much you make service a part of your church culture, as long as you have Christians coming in from other churches, you're going to have to retrain them. They'll come in with the preconceived notion that the pastor and staff are paid employees to serve them, not that it's our job to prepare them for service."

"They pay us to get them to work. It does sound kinda strange."

"When you put it that way, it does. Anyway, it'll be a perpetual challenge. And you'll have some people who just don't want to get involved. Sue Mallory taught us that it's worship plus two. We caught on to that and teach it in our membership class and newcomer materials."

"What's 'worship plus two'?"

"Sorry. It means we want you involved in regular worship, plus a place where you are using your gifts to serve others, plus a place where you're receiving service from others and where you're developing spiritually, such as a small group."

"Worship plus two. That's good."

"Keep it simple. It's easier to remember that way. A lot of people who'll come to your church will either be hurting or burned out, so they need a place to renew themselves as they serve."

"What about timeouts or sabbaticals? If someone's burned out, is it OK just to sit and refresh?"

"It's hard for me to see an experienced, talented person sitting on the sidelines; but yeah, sometimes people do just need a rest. Give people time, but use your Ministry Connectors to follow up with them regularly. This will remind people they're cared for, and will encourage them to come back to service as soon as they're ready."

Vernon looked at his notes. "Oh, here's another idea. We realized there were a number of people who didn't want an ongoing ministry commitment. Maybe they traveled or were senior adults who didn't feel comfortable doing long-term, consistent ministry. We started a group called Whatever It Takes. They use the acronym WIT."

"How's that work?"

"If we have special events or a big task, such as collating our annual State of the Church report, or perhaps need help hosting a group coming through, we call this team, and they show up and love it. The key is finding out what people love doing and can do, and then tailor-fit the ministry around them and their schedules."

"Sounds like that one takes some coordination."

"It does, but that's what your equipping team is for, to help establish leaders of the WIT ministry who then coordinate their team members. That's why, like I said before, if I had one thing to do over again, I'd be sure to have the equipping ministry leader on board as soon as possible."

"**C**hurch change doesn't need to be an oxymoron," Vernon said, smiling at Matt. "But it's close."

"This equipping emphasis has already started to affect our church," Matt said. "I've started talking with various key leaders. But there's some hesitation when I describe what I envision happening at Crossroads and hint at my role changing as pastor."

"That's to be expected. Think about how your frustration prepared you for our conversations; but even then, you've been processing this for a few months now. Let me show you something that really helped me." Vernon tore a sheet of paper from his leather folder and put it on the table. He wrote what looked like some sort of formula.

$$\frac{(\text{Leader Umph}+\text{Congregational Readiness})\times\text{Time Speed}}{\text{Idea Impact}} = \begin{array}{l}\text{Transition}\\\text{Index}\end{array}$$

Vernon continued. "Several years ago, I attended a conference that Gene Appel hosted, while he was still pastor at Central Christian Church near Las Vegas. He's now at Willow Creek. But Gene and a couple of other guys wrote a book called *How to Change Your Church Without Killing It*. At the time, I swore I should write a book, *How to Kill Your Church Without Changing It*."

The two men laughed.

"Yeah, or *How to Change Your Church Without Letting It Kill You*," Matt said.

Vernon laughed. "Anyway, one of the authors shared this formula that really helped me, so I use it to explain change to pastors. I won't go into all the details, but here's a recap that will give you an idea of how you want to go about it. The bottom line is that you'll need to have two plans. Basically one that says, 'here's *what* we want to do,' meaning becoming an equipping church; and the second one that says, 'here's *how* we want to do it.' This should include a transition plan for getting from where you are now to where you want to be."

"Why do I need two plans?"

"Because most good ideas of significance don't make it in church, not because the ideas are flawed, but because we underestimate the inertia in our church. Many churches just resist change—good or bad.

"So change is more about what happens externally, physically, and logically. Transition is about what happens internally, emotionally, and relationally. Transition is what helps people prepare for change. That's why a lot of people resist new ideas—because leaders have not prepared them to receive those ideas."

"So what does this formula have to do with change?"

"Well, there are primarily four key factors that influence any change. I have an article I'll e-mail you. It shows you how to estimate the value of each of key factors, work some simple math, and come up with an index that tells you how your change process might work in your church."

"That would be great."

"Here's a fast overview of the four key factors. *Leader Umph* is basically how gifted the pastor is in leading. On a 5-point scale, most of us are probably ones and twos by nature, because we have other strengths that reflect our pastoral calling. There aren't a lot of fours and fives out there, which makes initiating change more difficult for us."

"So is there hope?"

"Oh sure, but it means we have to rely more heavily on understanding the other three factors. The problem is when pastors think they're stronger leaders than they are and, as a result, try to charge forward without realizing the consequences of how these factors work together."

"That makes sense; OK."

"*Congregational Readiness* is really about where your opinion leaders stand or how they are apt to respond to the new idea. Again, you can estimate this on a 1 to 5 numeric scale and plug the numbers into the formula."

"By *opinion leaders* you mean people in your congregation who are formal leaders?"

"Really, people who are influencers, regardless of any position they may or may not hold. We talked about that a few months ago after the board meeting."

"I remember. So why don't you just do a congregational survey?"

"Two reasons. Because only 5 to 10 percent of your congregation pretty much determines what 80 to 90 percent of the others will respond to in terms of ideas. Five to 10 percent is a far more manageable number. Plus, you don't want to create a mess by telling everyone what you're thinking of doing before you've gotten them ready. Remember, the farmer prepares the soil to receive the seed, because he wants it to grow. Smart pastors invest a lot of time in preaching sermons on the equipping theme in order to lay a foundation, as well as reading key books on the topic with lay leaders, and taking strategic people with them to conferences or to visit churches that model equipping."

"That's good."

"The faster you go, the more stress it will create on your church, and thus lower the chances the change will be adopted. That's why in the formula you multiply with the *Time Speed* factor. It's explained in the article I'll send you."

"So how much time are we talking about?"

"Well, one to six months is like a microwave oven; one to two years is the equivalent of a conventional oven; and three to five years is similar to a crockpot. You can reduce the stress and increase the transition process by adding time, so long as you use the time to continually communicate and prepare people. Does that make sense?"

"It does. What's the last factor?"

"It's the *Idea Impact*, which in this case has to do with the equipping value. You want Crossroads to be a place where people grow spiritually by using their gifts. But the *Idea Impact* could be any number of things."

"So why is it on the bottom?"

"Because you divide by this factor. The smaller the impact the idea will have on the church, the better the chances of a positive transition. But the larger the impact an idea will have on a church, the more challenging the transition will be. By seeing how these four factors interact with each other, you can estimate how well your church will transition. If it looks like a bumpy road, then you can modify some factors—you can extend the time, or increase the readiness of your congregational influencers through discussion, books, and conferences, or you can reduce the amount of change you're proposing."

"So what if you decide to go through the change even if the formula warns you that you're at risk?"

"Well, like any good pilot, you instruct everyone to assume the crash position."

"And polish up the old résumé."

"Exactly, Matt. The problem is that unless you understand how organizations resist change by nature, you often work naively, and then wonder why you cause church splits or end up looking for a new job. The authors of that article suggested that in a significant change process, even a good one, you're apt to lose around 10 percent of your congregation."

"Wow, that's quite a bit."

"Yes, but if it's the right thing, you'll gain a lot more than that as a result."

"Sounds like a good article—that will save me some pain."

"I'll get it to you. I think it'll help you."

"So where do we go from here?"

"Well, I think we've probably covered enough yardage for now. I think it's up to you to continue processing and implementing it at Crossroads. I'd suggest we check in periodically for trouble-shooting, but you're ready to figure out what it's going to look like on your own."

"What, no diploma or commencement? Seriously, I really appreciate all you've done for me, Vernon. I don't have any doubt that this will not only change the way I do ministry as a pastor, but also how it will impact our church."

"Well, that's what we're here for, isn't it? To help people get better. We'll stay in touch, I'm sure, and you'll want to make sure that your director of equipping meets regularly with Chris—at least for a while. If we can help you avoid any potholes along the way, we'll be glad to do it."

The two pastors said goodbye to each other on the coffee shop patio. Even though his "course" on equipping ministry was coming to a close, Matt knew he'd gained a new friendship. Little did he know that day he wearily sat down next to Vernon how much the pastor would teach him…and how much it would change his life, his ministry, and the people at his church.

(You can read or download a free article, "Effective Church Transitions" by going to www.rev.org. Click on Me to We and then "Church Change.")

principle

A congregation needs a variety of systems to effectively implement the equipping value so that it becomes a part of the church culture.

THE
PRIZE

choppy seas

s.o.s.

gains and losses

the s-curve 'trough'

progress

momentum

blessed

Choppy Seas

"**Y**ou're serious about this, aren't you?" Ben, the part-time youth pastor of Crossroads, exclaimed. "I thought this was about recruiting more volunteers to help us, not turning over our ministry to them."

"What do you mean?" Matt said. "We've been talking about this for months."

"I know, but, well…"

"You didn't think I'd stick with this, is that what you mean?"

"I don't know. I'm all for having laypeople help, but what you're talking about doesn't seem feasible: to turn over ministry to people who haven't been trained and have so many other priorities distracting them. I just don't think it's realistic to expect laypeople to have the commitment we need to sustain a viable youth ministry."

"Glenn, what about you?" Matt asked. Glenn was the part-time worship leader at Crossroads. The tall, late-30s man fidgeted, as if unsure of how to answer.

"To be honest, I have some doubts. I'm not sure about the biblical precedent for this either," Glenn said, softly. "I went to college to be professionally trained as a worship leader. Do you think I should have people who've not been professionally trained and who don't have experience in leading worship to rotate in during our Sunday morning services as the worship leader?"

"What we've been saying is that our role as pastors needs to change, from being the primary ministry doers to training and empowering others to take active roles in ministry," Matt answered. "If you find someone who has the potential to lead in worship, then yes, I'd expect you to develop that person or people and then give them opportunities to lead."

"Wow, that just seems pretty risky, when you have so much riding on such a key portion every week," Glenn said. "I don't see how it can happen, realistically."

"Donna, how about you?" Matt asked. Donna, a fortysomething woman, leaned forward in her chair. She'd been the full-time administrative assistant for several years.

"Well, if you remember, I started as an office volunteer," she said. "So I don't have anything against unpaid people in the church office. I'm just not sure what this has to do with me because I'm not a pastor, and I have a pretty full schedule already. I don't have time to be managing volunteers in addition to what I'm doing now. Plus, what happens when you depend on someone, and the person has out-of-town guests or decides to do something else at the last minute? When you rely on people and they drop the ball, either what needed to get done doesn't, or you end up working twice as much yourself."

Matt nodded support, contemplating what to say next. He felt disappointed and somewhat frustrated with what he was hearing. Vernon had told him about this potential challenge, but Matt hadn't thought his staff would balk at the idea since they were a less traditional church than Westover. Besides, the paid staff had been included in the ministry leadership meetings the last few months. Everyone seemed to embrace the idea initially, but now that it was time to implement the value, Matt felt surprised by the resistance.

"We're all new at this," Matt said. "I don't have all the answers, but we need to model this value at Crossroads, if we want our congregation to embrace it and know that we're serious about it."

"Maybe what bothers me is the shift," Ben said. "I mean, none of this was mentioned when I was hired a year and a half ago. So if I'm going to be honest, in a way, I feel like you're changing things on us after the fact, to do something we weren't hired to do. I'm not trying to be rude or disrespectful, but I'm not sure how the youth will respond to a bunch of laypeople running their program. We've been a pretty tight group up to now."

"I'm asking you to try," Matt said. "I'd like us to talk about it in our weekly staff meetings, and we'll help each other figure it out."

"If you can cut back a bit on some of the things I'm doing now, it would help me," Donna said. "I just can't spend time training and scheduling office volunteers, while I'm doing all I am."

"I understand," Matt said. "We'll all have to do that awhile as we get started."

"I don't know," Glenn cautioned. "When you're talking about an area like the worship arts, that's pretty talent intensive. I think you're asking for trouble when you expand the circle and start having new people involved. I can't think of anyone now who could do what I do, with any level of competence."

"Well, that's a part of all our jobs, from this point out," Matt said. "To find and train people and give them a try. We'll never know if we don't let people have a chance to show what they have. Let's pray that God opens our eyes to how we can accomplish this."

Glenn slowly shook his head and pursed his lips.

"I'll try," Ben said. "I guess I can think about more of a team approach, but it may take awhile to get people trained and onboard. I don't think it's going to be as easy as it sounds up to now in our discussions."

"You know, I agree with you," Matt said. "Talking about it is a lot easier than actually doing it. I do think that if we help each other, we can figure out how to get this going in each of our areas. I'm trying to find someone who'll be the point person for this ministry as well, so I'm experiencing some of the same things as you are. Donna, if you can find a team of a half a dozen or so people who'll help us administratively in the office, that would be great."

"I don't know," Glenn said. "I'd hate to try this and have it turn out to be a fad or something we end up not doing, and have it set us back. Recovering is never easy."

"I understand that risk," Matt said, forcing a smile. "I still think we should try, because I believe God is calling us to move in this direction."

After the meeting, the three staff members left Matt's office. Matt closed the door. The optimism and encouragement he'd mustered in the meeting quickly evaporated. He plopped in his desk chair and slumped down. *What in the world was I thinking?* he thought to himself. *This isn't going to be as easy as I thought. It sounded so much simpler when Vernon described it.*

"**I** 'm sorry, Matt, Pastor Miller is away on his study leave," the ministry assistant said over the phone. "But he's checking his e-mail occasionally, so you might get hold of him that way."

"All right, thanks then," Matt said, hanging up the phone. He swiveled his chair to his laptop and began tapping an e-mail:

—————Original Message—————
From: Matt Robinson
Sent: Tuesday, May 11, 3:49 PM
To: Vernon Miller
Subject: S.O.S.

S.O.S. S.O.S. The ship is sinking!

Sorry to bug you on your leave, but we're having some rough sailing here. The staff isn't buying into implementing our impetus on equipping. I know we talked about this early on, but any additional advice?

Matt

—————Original Message—————
From: Vernon Miller
Sent: Tuesday, May 11, 4:49 PM
To: Matt Robinson
Subject: Re: S.O.S.

Matt, you may take on some water, but this won't sink your boat. You're going to make it. What can I do for you? I remember our early days, trying to convince staff, our ministry assistants, and even a few of our board members. They need some time. Assume that early negativity or pushback is more about fear than it is logical or doctrinal.

Remember the triangle on why people fail in a task? Think education and info more than heart and motives. Assume the best for now and keep moving forward. I'm good to e-mail, so keep in touch that way.

Vernon

―――――Original Message―――――
From: Matt Robinson
Sent: Wednesday, May 12, 9:13 AM
To: Vernon Miller
Subject: Thanks!

Whew, thanks, Vernon. Appreciate the encouragement. I think my initial e-mail was that emotional jolt you feel after a tough board meeting or counseling session that goes awry. Feeling a little better right now after a night's sleep, but still wanting to make sure that our leaders are onboard with this sea change. I'm not sure if I realized the initial challenge. I think it's much easier to do, just you and me at Starbucks.

Matt

―――――Original Message―――――
From: Vernon Miller
Sent: Wednesday, May 12, 10:01 AM
To: Matt Robinson
Subject: Re: Thanks!

LOL, very true, but isn't all of life? It's good for you to discuss it, in a coaching style, in your weekly staff meetings and one-on-ones. The latter is important so you don't embarrass someone who may be lagging a bit and so the individual doesn't infect others with a negative bug. You know how that goes. Look for little things to compliment them on—baby steps toward progress that rewards what you want to see more of.

The bottom line is that you're going to have to live in the tension as you transition. Sorry I can't be there to chat in person. I have to admit, the inspiration of the mountains and Scriptures were just what this old soul needed to refresh myself. Sounds like you may need some kind of getaway like this. Leaders need to care for their own souls during times of change, so don't let your fuel tank go dry.

Vernon

−−−−−Original Message−−−−−
From: Matt Robinson
Sent: Wednesday, May 12, 10:45 AM
To: Vernon Miller
Subject: Good wisdom

Good wisdom. Thx. One thing came up in a conversation I had last night after one of our gift-discovery workshops. Someone hinted that when people discover their gifts, this might become a problem when a ministry need arises. People might say, "Sorry, that's not my gift. Find someone else." How do you handle this? Sometimes you just need warm, willing bodies—not necessarily gifted ones.

Matt

−−−−−Original Message−−−−−
From: Vernon Miller
Sent: Wednesday, May 12, 2:01 PM

To: Matt Robinson

Subject: Re: Good wisdom

Matt, good question, a common one, too. Our goal is to help people find an ongoing ministry that matches their sweet spot. This is where they're most apt to be effective, feel fulfilled, and will sacrifice the most without complaining. We also teach that everyone is called to do things we don't necessarily enjoy, because we're made to serve. But we intentionally strive to make sure these are short-term commitments meaning we're filling gaps as we're looking for people who are gifted in that area. The church's job is to find serving opportunities that coincide with people's gifts, not find people who can fill our needs. It's a mind-set change in leadership for this to happen.

One time I heard a story about David Livingston, the famous African missionary and doctor. A log was stuck as they were building a hospital outpost in Africa. He called over to a man who was sitting nearby, reading a book. Livingston asked, "Can you help?" The man answered, "No, I'm an intellectual." Livingston said, "I tried that once. It didn't work." Livingston returned to moving the log. Was Jesus "gifted" at washing feet? Probably not, but there were dirty feet, so it needed to be done. At Westover, we try to teach the 80/20 rule here. Invest 80 percent of your ministry effort in the area of your strengths, and 20 percent where you're simply needed.

I was talking to Erik Rees, a guy at Saddleback who works in this area. He told me something like 50 to 60 percent of people in churches say they never use their gifts and skills in their ministry roles. That's not good stewardship. No wonder most churches hurt for workers and have less than a quarter of their people in serving. OK, that's probably more than you wanted; I'm rambling now. Need to let you go and get back to my study prep. Keep the faith.

Vernon

—————Original Message—————

From: Matt Robinson

Sent: Wednesday, May 12, 10:14 PM

To: Vernon Miller

Subject: Re: Re: Good wisdom

Thanks for the wisdom. There's so much to learn. I feel like you've given me an incredible launchpad, but I feel like a toddler with all this. My training hasn't prepared me for this kind of ministry.

Matt

——-Original Message——-

From: Vernon Miller

Sent: Thursday, May 13, 6:04 AM

To: Matt Robinson

Subject: Re: Re: Re: Good wisdom

Stay teachable, as you are, and you'll do fine. Humility is a prerequisite for learning and growing. Remember, your biggest challenge is to find the right person who'll develop an equipping team. Don't oversee the details yourself. Even though practically none of us as pastors have been trained to do this, in some ways, we're far more ready than we know. Like we said earlier, when pastors lower the bar in their calling and become the sole or primary ministry talent, they reduce their impact. Good coaches and teachers are more valuable than individual players and students, because they're multiplying themselves by developing others. Keep working on your self-image, moving from emperor to empowerer, and adder to multiplier. It'll happen.

Vernon

————Original Message————

From: Matt Robinson

Sent: Thursday, May 13, 10:14 AM

To: Vernon Miller

Subject: Great advice!

Hey, great advice! Really appreciate it. I'll try not to bug you anymore on your leave. Let's connect in a few weeks. Thanks again.

Matt

————Original Message————
From: Vernon Miller
Sent: Thursday, May 13, 10:18 AM
To: Matt Robinson
Subject: Re: Great advice

No worries. You're welcome.

Vernon

Gains and Losses

"Hey, what's the news at Crossroads?" Vernon asked, taking a sip from his to-go cup. "It's been a couple of months since we touched base. I think it was that S.O.S. distress call. See, you didn't sink."

Matt and Vernon laughed.

"Yeah, because you threw me a life preserver. What's this?" Matt asked, pointing to the lid on Vernon's cup. "I thought you liked the ceramic mugs."

"Oh, I guess even old dogs can learn new tricks. In fact, come to think of it, you've been working on behaving differently. How's your retooling going?"

"Well, good and bad, I guess. I was thinking the other day, it's been about a year since we began meeting. In fact, we ran into each right over there." Matt nodded to a table in the corner of the café.

"That's right. Wow, it's been a year already? That's scary, the way time flies. So as you stand back and look over the course of the year—where you were then and where you are now—what's working and what's not?"

"Good question. I like your coaching. Well, to be honest, I'd say that it's been a lot more work than I imagined."

"How so?"

"I had no idea how difficult it would be to change the way people think about me as pastor. It's not been easy retraining them, in spite of a lot of time and energy invested in the church leadership, along with getting our two directors trained. By the way, we only have one now…"

"What happened?"

"Well, there were Nancy and Sonya, but Sonya's husband got a job transfer, so they ended up moving to Florida. Just when we were building some steam in the equipping ministry."

"I hate when that happens. Well, just consider it a kingdom win, wherever she ends up in ministry."

"You're right. The workshops and new member classes have been really effective, and we had a lot of initial interest after this last fall message series on serving."

"That's good."

"But it's so laborious. Sometimes I think we're making great headway, and then the very next week, something happens where I think we'll never get there."

"Like what?"

Matt pondered silently. "Well, for instance, you told me never to do ministry alone. So I've now got a team of people we've designated as the congregational care team. They provide what used to be pastoral care, which includes hospital calls, praying with people, coordinating others to have meals delivered for people recovering from surgery or a new baby. Things like that. Well, it's been a bear trying to get this team going. I'll arrange my schedule to meet someone at the hospital, and then they call at the last minute and have to cancel. I end up doing the call alone. Or someone will tell me that they're going out of town for the weekend and can't follow up on a task, 'so could you fill in for me this time, Pastor?' I may as well be doing it myself. It's faster and easier that way."

Vernon sat, seemingly unmoved by Matt's plight.

"You don't seem to be phased by what I'm saying," Matt said.

"I'm not," Vernon answered. "I don't mean to sound insensitive, but nothing you're experiencing sounds significantly different than what I and every pastor I know, who's tried to take this seriously, have undergone. I think it's great you're making progress. This takes time. Remember, you're not starting a *program*. This is a long-haul *process* to change your church culture. Think marathon, not sprint. As much as possible, try to avoid rescuing people and work as hard as possible not to revert back to the old ways of doing things because they're easier. Of course they'll be easier, initially, just as it's more convenient following a worn path than carving a new one."

"But I can't just ignore someone in the hospital when they call. Oh, sorry Mr. Frank. The person scheduled to pray with you just flaked out. I'm sure your heart surgery will go just fine. Have a nice day."

"Man, you are stressed, aren't you?"

"You got me into this. Now get me out."

"Matt, it's about doing the right things over and over. Each time, you gain an inch. Inches become feet, and feet become yards, and yards become miles. Pretty soon you look back and see, 'Wow, I'm making progress.'"

"Seems like I take two steps forward and three back."

"Yeah, change is a big head game, isn't it? Well, let's look at your progress. How many of your 'discover your gifts' classes have you had? You called them *Happy Our*, right?"

"That's right. You envied the name, remember? Six, I think. They've been pretty well attended, I guess because people are curious and we're promoting them quite a bit the last few months."

"OK, that's great. So how is the staff doing in accepting this new approach to ministry?"

"The jury's still out. I think our office manager is onboard and our youth pastor. But I'm not sure about our worship guy."

"OK, well, that's two out of three. That's good. How's Carmen responding to all this?"

"Oh, you know, for the most part she's pretty positive. She's hoping for some light at the end of the tunnel, you know, helping me find more balance in life."

"Good, good. How's the board?"

"I'm not sure. It depends when you take their temperature, it seems. Sometimes you can see the excitement in their eyes about being able to lead. At other times, they seem overwhelmed. I wonder if they think if I'm doing my job. For the most part, though, I think they've bought into the concept. A couple of them have really stepped up in terms of leading, and I'm feeling pretty comfortable. I trust them, so far. A couple of others joined our two equipping ministry staff at the first-level training in Colorado. They came back really jazzed."

"That's great. What about the system?"

"System?"

"You know, the way you follow up on people, making sure they don't get overlooked, and making sure they receive proper training and orientation when they accept the invitation to the new ministry role."

"Oh, well, that's where I think we're a little behind. We're using paper forms with handwritten comments and sticky notes. But we're starting to figure out how to keep these up on the computer."

"Your equipping team is, right?"

"Yes, definitely—that's not my forte."

"Good. That one is really key but also very involved. Unless you've got a whiz-bang computer person and follow-up team, that's usually a hiccup in the process.

Keep coaching your equipping partner and her team. Figure out the best balance of being simple but also effective. You don't want to overbuild the system and make it complicated, but you also don't want to get stuck with one that just doesn't do the job. Try to avoid multiple databases where you have to replicate data entry. I'm not that attuned to the details at Westover. I'd encourage you to be aware but not get sucked into that process. People with different gifts than we have can figure this out."

Matt chuckled. "I need to keep reminding myself of that. It's so tempting to push everything aside and stick to whatever it is that's on my plate for the week."

"That's because we pastors have been taught to be firefighters, reactors. One reason this work is so difficult is because for the most part, it's proactive. You're laying the foundation for a skyscraper, not a barn."

"I have to keep telling myself that."

"You have enough going on, between sermon prep, counseling, and normal pastoral duties, that you have to stay very intentional in all of this. Keep the vision fresh. Talk it up in every meeting you're in with your staff and board. When you think you've beaten the drum to death, do it some more."

"I need to hear that."

"Did you ever figure out how many of your people were serving initially, so that you have a benchmark to see how you're progressing? You know, before you started your training classes."

"Oh, yes, we did. We estimated that we had approximately 18 percent of our active attendees in some kind of ministry at the time."

"Good, that's not a bad start. So in another six months, when you've been equipping for about a year, you'll want to survey again, maybe even sooner. We try to do it twice a year. That will give you a better feel of your progress. I'd also compare other measurements at that time, with the year previous, such as financial giving, attendance, small group involvement, and the like."

"Yeah, right now, it just seems like we're fighting a lot of fires and irritating some of our core people, and not seeing a lot of payoff. There are those moments I think it would be easier just to get out of the game."

The S-Curve 'Trough'

"**A**re you familiar with the *S-curve?*" Vernon asked.

"I don't think so," Matt said.

"It's better known in business circles, I think, but it's applicable in a lot of arenas." Vernon took out his paper pad, clicked his pen, made a broad curve like a distorted S, and then put numbers 1 through 7 at various locations on it.

"Matt, nearly every organization, project—and even our lives—goes through a life cycle that reflects an S-curve. Solomon explained it in Ecclesiastes 3 when he said there's a time for everything: a time to be born, a time to die, a time to build, and a time to pull back. Anyway, at point 1, it's the time for dreaming. This is like when you find out your wife is pregnant, or you begin brainstorming an innovation, or you come to a new church. It's a time of excitement and idealism."

Vernon continued. "Then, reality hits; point 2. You have your first worship service but instead of 200 people showing up, you have 80. It's the 2 a.m. feeding, or year two of a new pastorate, when you realize that whatever it is that you were dreaming about is going to be harder than you thought."

"I think that's where we're at now."

"I think you're right. That's pretty typical of this stage in a new venture."

"Oh great. That's like saying it's perfectly normal to be crazy, because insanity runs in your family."

"No, I'm saying it's to be expected. The good news is that if you persevere, you begin to make progress and see some growth and results of your hard work; point 3. Then if you continue to restructure, more growth takes place, point 4, and you start enjoying the fruit of your hard work—whether it's a business, marriage, kids, or exercise program. That's point 5 on the S-curve. Then eventually you'll begin to lose momentum, point 6, and decline will eventually set in, leading to death, point 7."

"So can you avoid death, I mean, in an organization or church?"

"Not without intentional intervention. The problem is that this has to start at point 5 if it's going to be most effective, just the time when you're feeling good about things and are tempted to relax. A lot of churches and denominations today are at point 6 on this curve. Many of them will not survive because they've all but lost their window for renewal."

"That makes a lot of sense, but it's kind of sad."

"That's why throughout history, God tends to bring renewal by starting new things. It's the new wine, old wineskin concept. It's easier to give birth than to raise the dead."

Matt laughed.

"My point to all this," Vernon continued, "is to encourage you that what you're feeling now is pretty typical." Vernon turned the paper toward him as he added something to it. He put a short line at the bottom of the curve, wrote the word "exit" and then drew a circle around that section.

"All right, that's an overview of the S-curve, but you need to understand the potential danger in the section you're in during this change initiative. Just as a new venture, idea, or innovation begins at point 1, the biggest threat comes at point 2, what I call *the trough*. That's the place where you face your first real problems. It's when people begin questioning your new idea. You don't have much or any success yet, so there's little payoff, making it more difficult to convince people that

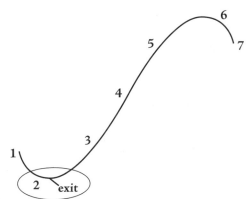

the new way is better than the existing. You may feel depressed, tired, and stressed."

"That's where I think we're at. That's where I'm at, anyway."

"You probably are. The danger of *the trough* is the temptation to give up. That's where most people *exit* a new idea, because it's easier than pushing through it. Nearly everything in life has *the trough*. It's where people decide to get out of a marriage because it's too tough, or close the doors on the new church or business, or where a person decides it's just not worth it and pulls the plug on the new venture. For the children of Israel, it's when they decided to head for the wilderness instead of the Promised Land in Numbers 14."

"So what are you saying about our context at Crossroads?"

"I'm saying that when you're in the trough, it feels like the best solution is to just quit, to go back to ministry as usual. You feel like the price isn't worth paying and the chaos isn't going to go away. The children of Israel said, 'Let's go back to Egypt.' Hey, even Jesus asked 'if it is possible, may this cup be taken from me. Yet not as I will, but as you will.' "

"We're there! I mean, I'm wondering if it's really worth it."

"Nearly every worthwhile venture in life has a trough. It doesn't mean you shouldn't quit, pull the plug, or consider the viability of a new idea. But if you quit, you'll never get to points 3 through 5. That's where you experience the payoff of the risk, the investment, and the struggle. It's when your baby begins sleeping through the night, when your new business begins to make a profit. It's the Promised Land, flowing with milk and honey. It's the Resurrection."

"You can preach that?"

"Absolutely. It's a great message of hope: the power of persevering. But I'm telling you now because I'd hate for us to meet six months from now and for you to tell me that you gave up pursuing this equipping value."

"So you went through this at Westover?"

"We did, and one thing that helped was that I'd learned this principle before going through it. When I was a young pastor, Ray and Anne Ortlund took me and my wife under their wings and mentored us. Ray and Anne are a seasoned pastor and wife who've invested in a lot of church leaders. So I'm just passing on what helped us as a young pastor and wife, when we were going through some early bumps in our ministry."

"That means a lot. I needed to hear that right now. So does every trough lead to milk and honey?"

"No, but many do. The problem is that if you take the exit, you'll never know. The other problem is that the more often you use the exit, the more you'll be tempted to take it the next time and the next. It's why some people move from job to job and why second and third marriages have higher failure rates than first ones."

"So you're saying we need to persevere."

Vernon smiled. "You do. I'm convinced there's a Promised Land for you and Crossroads—if you persevere and if you apply the things we've discussed over the last year or so. You're facing the giants now, but the milk and honey will come."

Matt rested his chin in his hands with his elbows on the table. He stared into Vernon's eyes. "Tell me it's worth it. Tell me the chaos we're feeling right now will make sense someday and we'll be glad we went through this."

"If I were a betting man, I'd wager a Venti Caramel Macchiato on it."

Matt leaned back and laughed. "Well at those prices, I guess that's as much of a guarantee as I'm going to get, isn't it?"

"You can take it to the bank."

"OK, we'll keep at it."

"Hey, Vernon, how are you?" Matt asked, calling Vernon on his cell. "It's been a couple of years now since we launched our equipping emphasis at Crossroads, thanks to your guidance. I thought we could go out to dinner, catch up a bit. My buy."

"Ah, my two favorite words, *my buy*," Vernon said with a chuckle. "Let's do it. How's your budget? Shall we invite our wives as well?"

"Sounds good," Matt said.

+ + +

"That was good food," Vernon said. "I really like this place."

"We like it, too," Matt said. "It's one of our favorites. We just wanted to say thanks again for all the help you've been in our transition. After all, you taught me that celebrating and recognition are important elements to an equipping church."

"That is true," Vernon said. "We don't do that enough in ministry, do we?"

"Celia, we really appreciate your husband's time and effort," Matt said.

"Oh, he's so impressed with the way you've grabbed onto this different way of ministry," she replied. "You're doing a difficult but very important thing. I remember a lot of late nights and early mornings when Vernon was leading Westover through this process."

"So how long should this take?" Carmen asked. "I mean, I know it's an ongoing process, but it still feels sort of chaotic. Chaotic isn't the right word. I guess it's more like undone or unproven."

"Well, it is a process," Vernon said. "But there does come a time when it 'kicks in,' when you begin to sense a convergence of your hard work. I think of it as harvest time. Growing up in Iowa, after a long time working the fields and waiting, the corn would ripen to the point that Dad would say, 'OK, it's time. Let's pick corn.'"

"We're not there yet," Matt said. "But we are seeing some good progress. We have nearly half of our adults through the gifts and assessment process and have nearly twice as many people involved in a ministry; right around 35 percent."

"Thirty-five percent? That's incredible," Vernon said, loudly. "If I remember, you had less than 20 percent when you started. That's great progress. You're obviously doing some things right."

Carmen said, "I wasn't trying to be negative. What I meant was, how long does it take before you don't have to push it so much? It seems like we're constantly talking about it and weaving it into sermons, announcements, and small groups."

"Chances are you'll always have to do that to an extent," Vernon said. "It's the same reason we talk about love, forgiveness, prayer, and worship. Vision leaks. It just sort of evaporates amid all the other things vying for people's attention. If it's an essential, you have to bring it up over and over, hopefully in new and interesting ways. I think what you're asking is when does equipping become a part of the church culture, so people come to expect it as a way of life at Crossroads."

"I think that's what I mean," Carmen said.

"It will take a good three to five years," Vernon said. "In spite of your great progress, you're probably not there yet."

"I remember when it seemed we were living and breathing this," Celia said. "One of the mistakes Vernon made, or at least he says he made, was that he let up on the accelerator after getting things going. The launch is important, but you can't let up after it."

"Someone once told me, 'If you want the caboose to get to the station, the engine has to pass the station,'" Vernon said. "That means you have to go further than you think. Even though you and your core leaders may be living and breathing this value, there are still probably a lot of people in your church who haven't taken this seriously."

"Some of them are waiting to see how seriously you're going to take it," Celia added.

Matt asked, "So in spite of all our work, the caboose isn't to the station yet?"

Vernon chuckled. "This isn't for the fainthearted. You're not only redefining your congregation, you're changing as a pastor as well. That takes time, too."

"I hadn't thought about that," Matt said. "That's true. I'm probably learning as much or more about what it means to pastor in an empowering approach. I still feel like I'm pretty busy."

"That's true. I thought the equipping value was supposed to make his work lighter," Carmen said.

"I think that question should be, are you busy because you're still doing ministry yourself or are you busy because you're transitioning from a traditional model to an equipping one?"

"What do you mean?" Matt asked.

"I mean that you're probably still in a transition phase," Vernon explained. "You're not fully vested in the new paradigm, and you haven't left the old one, so you're straddling both," Vernon said.

"That makes sense," Carmen said. "It feels like that, even though if I may say so, he's doing far better at not doing things himself. We've seen a lot of new people getting involved in ministry teams."

"That's exciting, isn't it?" Celia asked.

"It is," Carmen said.

"How's your search for a new worship leader going?" Vernon asked.

"I think it's going well," Matt said. "We've got it down to two candidates, and we're really trying hard to investigate how well they do at team-building."

"Good," Vernon said. "That's a key position. It's too bad your worship guy didn't buy into the team approach. The star syndrome is more common than we'd like to admit in ministry. You're looking for a different kind of leader."

"We are," Matt said. "The good part is that some of our worship team has really stepped up in the interim. We probably don't have anyone on the team who can take over, but we've been quite surprised at who has come forward as well as the amount of talent that we didn't know we had."

Vernon smiled. "That's what happens when people catch the vision. Imagine what it would be like if every church began mining the talent and potential in them."

"But we thought we had been," Carmen said. "How can churches know they're not reaching their potential, even when they're begging and pleading for help every week? You think you're getting all people have to give."

"That's very deceiving, isn't it?" Vernon said. "It's like the tip of the iceberg. We think we're tapping our potential because we get up on Sunday mornings during the service and plead for help, with minimal results. But creating an equipping environment is a significantly different approach to ministry. It's like operating a farm, not just going to the grocery store. It's like mining for gold, not just walking into a jewelry store. The process is a lot more involved, but the results are significantly greater as well. You can't do that with a 40-day program, a sermon series, or spiritual gifts workshop here and there."

"But it's so worth it," Celia affirmed. "I hope you stay with it, because although it's very messy getting there, the result really is what we'd always longed for in the pastorate. We'd never go back to the old way of doing ministry."

"That's good to hear," Matt said. "Sometimes you wonder if it's worth it."

"We just need to persevere, honey," Carmen said. "You're doing a good job. We're just not there yet."

"What are the places you feel like you're either stuck or that aren't working well?" Vernon asked.

"I guess sometimes you don't know what you don't know," Matt said. "But I'm thinking that we don't have all the systems worked out. We're still trying to get our arms around the whole data entry, follow through, and team-building process. We just recently began the exit interview process."

"What's that?" Carmen asked. "I haven't heard about that."

"It's when someone resigns or leaves a ministry; someone from the equipping team connects with the person to see why he or she left, and if possible, see if there might be a better fit in another ministry area," Matt explained.

"That's good," Vernon said. "Not only does it let people know you care, but many times helps people find a better place of service. And it lets you know if you have problems in a ministry area before it becomes significant. Retention problems usually indicate an underlying leadership issue."

"What do you mean?" Matt asked.

"Well, as you know, we monitor how many people are involved in our various ministries," Vernon said. "We noticed that our children's ministry staff kept shrinking. After awhile, our equipping director had a conversation with the children's pastor. The pastor told her that they didn't need as many workers. It was OK. When the director started asking questions among former ministry participants, it turns out that she wasn't doing any training, the meetings lacked team-building and excitement, and so people began drifting away. We had to intervene and help the children's pastor gain some new skills and be more accountable for ministry development."

"There's so much to do," Carmen said.

"If you do it right, there is," Vernon said. "That's why you can't do it alone. You have to do it as a team."

"I feel like we're doing a lot of things, but I'm not sure how many of them we're doing well," Matt said. "I mean, we really are progressing, but it still has to be very intentional."

"How's Nancy doing as the equipping director?" Vernon asked.

"She's great," Matt said. "She's really doing a great job helping people get connected."

"Just a reminder, she needs to focus on developing her team as much as possible, and invest in a handful of others who do what she does. Be sure she's modeling equipping herself, so that if anything happens to her, the team will continue," Vernon said.

"Good point," Matt said. "We could probably improve that."

"You have a lot going on," Vernon said. "That's to be expected. But it seems like you're in a much better place than you were a year ago."

Matt laughed. "Yeah, I see some light at the end of the tunnel—I mean, the end of the trough," he said.

"That's good," Vernon chuckled. "That exit door can be pretty tempting when you're transitioning a church. I'm glad you're doing well. Keep at it and when we do dinner again next year at this time, you'll have some great stories to tell."

"I'm thinking we should buy next time," Celia said.

"There's a great little Polynesian restaurant we like," Carmen said.

"Where's that?" Vernon asked.

"Honolulu," Carmen said. The couples laughed.

"What's it been, three years now?" Vernon asked.

"More like three and a half since we started talking," Matt said. "We just hit our three-year mark since beginning our transition toward an equipping oriented value at Crossroads."

"Wow, time flies," Vernon said. "So where are you at? I apologize for not staying in better touch the last few months."

"Oh, no problem. It's not your fault. I should have called sooner. Overall, it's going great. I can't believe I'm telling you this, after all the stormy days I've described the first couple of years. I think we're starting to get it."

"That's wonderful to hear. Tell me, what's going well?"

"We just finished our semiannual survey and we're just over 50 percent of our active attendees in some sort of service role."

"Half your people are using their gifts? That is amazing!" Vernon shouted. People in the coffee shop looked at the two men, but Vernon didn't seem to notice the attention. "Wow, that is great, Matt. How have you done it?"

"Like you said, we just keep working at it all the time. Actually, I'm loving it because less of my time now is spent on this. Nancy, our equipping director, has developed a great team, and she's really expanded the number with ministry connectors, admin, data entry people, and she's taken about a half-dozen others to the equipping training at Group in Loveland, Colorado. She actually talked me into joining them last year, so I went. It was great."

"That's so exciting. So how have you gotten that many people organized?"

"We just did what you told us. They've put together a great system. And I think—for the most part—they've worked out the bugs. It's a continual process, as you know, but they've pretty much honed their lines of communication and follow through," Matt paused and grinned sheepishly.

"Yeah?" Vernon asked.

"We're not just at 50 percent involvement," Matt said. "We've also grown about 50 percent in the last couple of years. We lost a few people, like you said we would. That was pretty hard, and some of the naysayers pointed that out, but they've been replaced by new people; and in general, the new attendees are more responsive to this idea of involvement."

"It's because you're training them early 'This is who we are at Crossroads.'"

"It's working. So not only do we have more people, percentage-wise, we have a lot more people total. We're starting to see greater ownership and finances are up as well."

Vernon raised his hand toward Matt for a high five. Matt slapped it.

"Wow," Vernon said.

Matt continued. "I'm starting to feel more of a rhythm, too, enjoying my preaching and teaching more, and preparing leader lessons like you showed me. There's definitely more of a joyful spirit around the church."

"What else?" Vernon asked, sensing Matt was having a hard time containing his enthusiasm.

"We've begun to think beyond our church walls. We have anywhere from 10 to 20 percent of our people who are serving outside of Crossroads. Right now, about half of them are doing both, inside and outside, but we have about a half-dozen different community agencies and projects that we promote internally that are not church programs."

"Impressive. And I should add, we enjoyed having your church join us in the citywide workday last month. I think we're up to 20 congregations doing that, and we hope to increase next year. In fact, it's become a separate 501.3C, so we're not officially in charge anymore."

"That's great. Our people really enjoyed it."

"Super, Matt. So is there anything you're wrestling with?"

"Oh sure. Like you said, there are still empty places where we're scrambling to fill the gaps, but it's not what it used to be. One interesting thing we've noticed is that when we get a good ministry team formed, and they begin making friendships and enjoying each other, sometimes it's tough for them to embrace new people into their group."

"Ah, that's interesting."

"Have you noticed that? For example, we have a group of ladies, really wonderful, who are on call to prepare meals for funerals, visiting guests, et cetera. They said they don't want any more help, and we've actually lost a couple of people who tried to join their ministry but felt like they were being excluded."

"Too much of a good thing, huh? That's interesting. Yes, we've noticed that as well at Westover. When ministry teams bond, sometimes it is more difficult to add new people."

"What do you do?"

"It's an ongoing issue, so we haven't fixed it. A couple of things help. One is that sometimes you may need a rotating commitment, so that after a year or two, a person takes half a year off to keep the team fresh and inviting. They can rotate back on, but by then the chemistry has changed a bit. That keeps it healthier and not so ingrown. Another thing we do is in our training. We're constantly talking about making new people feel welcomed and being sure the ministry connector creates bridges. We see it more in some areas than others."

"Great ideas," Matt said as he jotted a note on the pad of paper he had brought. "See, you've got me using this archaic recording device."

"Ah, ancient and future. Anything else you're wrestling with?"

"Oh, let's see. Yes, it seems like most of our people have been through our *Happy Our* seminar, so our attendance in these workshops has dropped off quite a bit. We're trying to think of some new ways to reach people who've not been through it yet, as well as continuing to emphasize it in our new member class."

"That's good. Matt. You probably will need to continually think of new ways to reach people, because after an idea has run its course or you've reached a certain saturation point, the previous approach won't cut it."

"That's good to hear. We're not discouraged, just trying to figure out how we can keep casting the vision and training people in new formats and venues."

"I'm trying to think of what we've done at Westover to keep people processing over the years. I remember we've had that same experience: sort of reaching a plateau. I know we still make a big deal about it in our membership courses, and I still do some one-on-ones with people who look like they may have leadership potential. That makes even more of an impact as your church grows, because face time with the pastor goes up in value—supply and demand."

"I am trying to do that. I used to feel intimidated by some of the leader types, but I've come to embrace them. We have a pastor's class now that is just for potential leaders, and we have about 10 at any given time."

Vernon laughed.

"What?" Matt asked.

"I am so proud of you. Listen to you. You've become an equipping pastor. Just three years ago you could hardly spell it and now you are one." The two men laughed.

"Well, you're to blame for that," Matt said.

"Nah, it was there all the time. All we did was discover what the Bible was trying to tell us. I just happened to be a step or two ahead of you on the trail."

O n the five-year mark of Pastor Robinson's venture into the equipping arena, he invited Pastor Miller to a breakfast at the nicest hotel in the city. It was a beautiful Monday morning. The sun shone on the two men as they sat outside on the patio.

"So tell me, how are things going?" Vernon asked.

"I don't know where to begin," Matt said. "It's a journey, you know that. We haven't arrived. But I honestly believe that Crossroads is a different church than it was five years ago. We've turned a corner, big time."

"Why do you say that?"

"There is so much energy in our church now. We're seeing more people than ever in leadership roles. It's not just the frazzled few, serving the consuming crowd."

"How many of your people are serving?"

"We're just under 70 percent," Matt said with a big smile.

"That's amazing! Truly fantastic."

"Not only that, we've more than doubled in size since we started this process. Actually, it's closer to a 150 percent increase. So we've added staff, the kind who train and equip others, I might add, and I've never had more fun doing what I do."

"See, I told you. I knew you'd do it."

"I know. I can't believe I get paid to do what I do. But don't tell my board."

"I won't tell your board if you don't tell mine. It's become a part of your church culture, hasn't it?"

"I think so. I mean in some ways, it still feels like we're just getting going. We have a lot to learn, but we really do embrace this value. People are taking ownership. We are seeing new visitors every week who tell us that they met someone from our church working in their neighborhood, or down at the homeless shelter, or building a Habitat house, or on a baseball team that one of our people coached. It's truly amazing."

"You're seeing what God can do through people who discover their gifts and purpose, aren't you?"

"It's amazing! The best part is that I'm freed up to do what I need to be doing, plus what I'm more gifted at. There are certain things that only the pastor can do, but at least now I'm not going crazy, chasing distractions. I kinda thought that when our church became an equipping church, I'd just sit around and drink tea or coffee and have nothing to do. My job is to keep us focused on our mission, the big picture. And my family is getting the best of me because I'm not constantly preoccupied, wondering what else I should be doing. When I'm home, I'm home. I'm not wondering what people are thinking about me for not being with them. I realize that having to do so many things that weren't my strengths was sucking the joy out of me."

"That's it. That's what I was trying to tell you in the very beginning when we met. The ministry is such a beautiful thing when you come to understand what it was really designed to be: To prepare people to do God's work, not to do it all yourself or think you're to do it. I think that's why so many pastors are leaving the ministry, because more and more, church complexities require them to do things that lay beyond their gifting, if they don't embrace the equipping value."

"I think you're right, Vernon. I never knew what I was missing. I guess I feel bad for all those pastors who feel like they never match the expectations they think they have to meet. It's like they're driving down the wrong road. I was one of those pastors."

Matt continued. "You know Jeff Engle?"

"He's the pastor at Eastside Chapel across town?" Vernon asked.

"Yeah, well, I got a call recently. He'd heard we were doing some neat things at Crossroads, so guess what I did?"

"Ah, here's a wild guess. You invited him to Starbucks?"

"And began mentoring him, just like someone I know."

"I'm really proud of you, Matt. It may be that the only thing we can do is try to model it ourselves, and come alongside other pastors and help them consider a different way of fulfilling their calling, one by one."

Vernon continued. "Perhaps our calling is twofold: to empower our congregation and to engage our colleagues in a different pastoral paradigm. So what's been challenging for you, as you look back over the five years?"

"Well, getting going really was a bear. You know those crazy calls and e-mails I made to you, but we persevered and tried to keep working at it. I was so used to doing programs that it was tempting to treat equipping this way and hype it up a few weeks at a time. But I think I learned how to cast the vision consistently, over the long haul, without making it just an emotional thing."

"That's right. It's a different approach."

"I think letting go was a big deal for me. I'm not running our board meetings. I'm not the sage on the stage, as we called it, in that we have several people telling their stories and even team preaching. My role has certainly taken more of a behind-the-scenes feel, but at the same time, I feel like I've never been more productive. It's so fun to see people brighten up, come alive."

Vernon nodded in agreement as Matt continued.

"In fact, that's probably the biggest single difference, besides the number of people involved, is the increase in spiritual growth I've seen the last couple of years. People seem more engaged in worship, and I catch these stories of people connecting faith to their everyday lives, unlike before. For example, a couple of weeks ago, I'm in the lobby after the service, people milling around. This guy came up to me and said, 'Pastor, I need a prayer.' So I thought, *That's great, he wants me to pray for him.* So I put my hand on his shoulder and began to bow my head. He says, 'No, I don't need you to pray for me, I need a prayer. I've been doing some carpentry work down at the halfway house, and one of the groups asked me to pray. Could you just write down something for me to say?' "

"That's funny."

"I know. Could I ever get a guy like that to come to a Bible study on prayer or a prayer seminar? No, but now that he's involved in helping people, who ask him to pray, he's open to learning about praying. When people get in real-life situations where they see how the Bible and God intersect with them, they're open to learning."

"Very cool, Matt."

"It is. The spiritual fruit I've seen, and the humility it has produced in so many of our leaders, is nothing short of amazing. For example, a few of our higher-octane businessmen started going down to a homeless center to tag along with their wives, maybe for safety or something. They started meeting some of the people, and now they're involved in fixing things and working with the city to get a building permit and more funding. Here are these successful businessman, driving downtown in their nice cars, washing dishes and playing catch with low-income kids in the parking lot." Matt paused, his eyes filling with tears. "It's nothing short of amazing."

Vernon smiled supportively. "So how are you able to do so many of these community projects? Who's running the ship?"

"Oh, we have a lot going on inside. But we've discovered that simple is better than complex. We've actually stopped doing some things that were just being done out of tradition, even though we're not very traditional, as you know. For example, you may know we used to do the big Walk-Through Christmas. But we realized that even though we were attracting a lot of people to the event, we were burning out our people, and it wasn't necessarily resulting in people growing spiritually or getting plugged into our church. So we quit it. We turned the same energy into getting people into community service during the holidays. Some people didn't like it, but over the long haul, it's been a great decision."

"Wow, that's impressive. Making those kinds of decisions isn't easy, but they are important. Good job."

"Another thing is that when we promote an event or need in the community, we get people coming up to a ministry leader saying, 'We'd prefer to work with this community project, so we'll be pulling out of our children's church commitment.' We'll have the children's ministry pastor coming to me and saying that we're stealing all their staff. It's an ongoing tension, but it reminds us that it's not about using people. It's about helping people find a place of meaningful ministry, whether it's inside Crossroads or outside."

"Wow, I'm so excited for you."

"Yeah, not long ago, the chief of police called me. I wasn't sure what he wanted. Turns out that he'd heard about what some of our people were doing down at the halfway house. He was so impressed that a church would do something like that, he asked if we'd be willing to host a community problem-solving group that was forming to brainstorm neighborhood issues. They meet at our church monthly now, with some very key people. Since I'm the host, I get to be a part of it, too. That contact alone has opened doors for spiritual conversations with people who'd never come to our Sunday worship services."

"Those are great stories, and you have to keep telling those stories. There's nothing that impacts a congregation more than hearing someone say how their life has been changed."

"That's true. And although I know that the main thing is for people to grow in their relationship with Jesus—which is happening, and it's not primarily to fill ministry slots—I have to tell you that it is *so* nice having a lot of people mobilized. I am no longer the first one in the building, setting up for a meeting, and the last one to leave because I'm cleaning up or locking the doors or feeling that I'm in charge. I'm like one of the rest of the people, doing my little part to build the kingdom."

Vernon chuckled. "That's a great side benefit, isn't it? You know, I'm convinced that the greatest satisfaction in life doesn't come from serving someone as much as it is in watching those you've prepared to serve, serve others. Maybe that's why being a grandparent is so rewarding. When you think about it, that's primarily how Jesus pastored."

The two pastors talked more. At the end of their time together, Matt reached into his computer bag and pulled out a flat, rectangular, gift-wrapped package. He cleared his throat.

"Vernon, I know that God works in strange and mysterious ways, his wonders to perform," Matt said, pausing as he felt his emotions rising. "Five years ago, we started out on a venture which has been nothing short of revolutionary for our church." Tears welled up in Matt's eyes. His voice broke. "I just want to tell you how much God used your wisdom, friendship, and advice to change my life and that of our congregation's." Matt handed the gift to Vernon.

"What's this?"

"Oh, it's just a token."

"Well, this breakfast was quite a reward in itself. What a wonderful setting."

"Hey, Starbucks is good, but this deserves a bit more pomp and circumstance."

Vernon slid his finger under the tape and opened the gift. He pulled a wooden plaque away from the paper and held it up so he could read the brass plate.

> **To my friend, colleague, and mentor**
>
> **Pastor Vernon Miller**
>
> **Who introduced me to God's call in my life**
>
> **To equip, prepare, and empower God's**
>
> **People for works of service,**
>
> **Resulting in many transformed lives.**
>
> **I'll be forever indebted.**
>
> **Pastor Matt Robinson**

principle

The pastor who perseveres to become an equipping pastor will experience personal benefits and will unleash the potential of the church.

We'd like to hear from you on how this book has impacted you
and/or what you're doing in your church to equip and empower others.
E-mail us at MeToWe@group.com.

Reflection
QUESTIONS

Reflections on the challenge

Reflections on the cost

Reflections on the Biblical Direction

Reflections on the Partnership

Reflections on the Plan

Reflections on the Prize

Reflection
QUESTIONS

Reflections on the Challenge

1. Why does a leader need to change personally before an organization can change significantly? What are some examples of this?

---

2. On a 1-to 5 scale, what are your feelings toward the status quo in your church?

1—**Quite happy** ☺	4—**Dissatisfied** ☹
2—**Comfortable** ☺	5—**In agony** ☹
3—**Ambivalent** 😐	

How does your choice affect your motivation for personal change?

---

3. What activities can you do to take your church to the next level? (For example, create a "Stop Doing List," or never do ministry alone.)

---

4. Pastors, like all Christians, do best when they invest at least two-thirds of their ministry time doing what they do best. List your top three gifts. Look at a typical week or month in your calendar—how much of your time do you spend using these three gifts?

Reflections on the Cost

1. Every change costs something. List three changes you'd personally like to make as a pastor, and list the potential "prices" associated with each one. (For example, if you choose to train others to do hospital calls instead of doing them yourself, it might cost you extra time at first and criticism for not calling on people yourself.)

The Change	The Cost

2. Think of critical decisions that have been made in the history of your church. What were the costs and benefits associated with each decision? Looking back, can you now say the beneficial results were worth the price? Why or why not?

Costs	Benefits

3. What is preventing you from paying the price for change and improvement—both in your personal life and in your ministry? How can you overcome those barriers?

4. How would your church respond if you became an equipper of ministers instead of the doer of ministry? What are the potential costs of doing this?

reflection
QUESTIONS

Reflections on the Biblical Direction

1. Describe Moses', Jesus', and Paul's models for pastoral ministry? How does the typical pastoral model differ from the way they did ministry?

_____

_____

_____

2. If you could ask Moses, Jesus, or Paul any question about how they did ministry, what would it be? Check out these Scriptures for clues: Exodus 18; Mark 6:30-44; Acts 20:13-36.

_____

_____

_____

3. On a scale of 1 to 5, how close are you to considering this new model of ministry?
   1. I'm definitely sticking to the traditional model at this point.
   2. I'm pretty good with the way we're doing things now.
   3. I'm not sure.
   4. I'm leaning toward a new way of doing ministry.
   5. I've already started!

4. What's the hardest part of giving up the traditional, pastor-centered paradigm?

_____

_____

_____

Reflection
QUESTIONS

Reflections on the Partnership

1. How could a partner help you champion the equipping value so your church embraces it fully?

_____

_____

2. List four members of your church who already reflect many qualities of a good equipping partner (for example: discernment, training skills, and organizational skills).

_____

_____

3. What one specific thing can you do this week to become less of an emperor and more of an empowerer? (For example, you might ask someone else to facilitate your board meeting, or you might use a coaching method in your next meeting with a ministry leader.)

_____

_____

4. How might your current church structure work for or against you as you begin implementing the equipping values? Are there policy changes or bylaws that need to be amended in order to help you implement these new values? If so, what are they, and how can you begin changing them?

_____

_____

reflection
QUESTIONS

Reflections on the Plan

1. Why is it important to have a plan as you begin implementing the equipping values in your church?

_____

_____

2. Why is it valuable for the pastor to understand the big picture but not be in charge of setting up and applying the various systems?

_____

_____

3. As you consider your church, what challenges will you face as you work to make equipping part of your church culture? How will you address those challenges in your plan?

_____

_____

4. Make a list of specific things you can do in the next six months to prepare your church to receive this new idea.

in 1 month: _____

in 2 months: _____

in 3 months: _____

in 4 months: _____

in 5 months: _____

in 6 months: _____

Reflections on the Prize

1. What did you learn in this chapter as Matt and Crossroads Church moved closer to an equipping model of ministry?

_____

_____

2. Describe a *trough* time in your life—when taking the *exit* was tempting. What did you do?

_____

_____

3. List three ways you think the equipping model would benefit you as a pastor. List three ways it would benefit your church.

_____

_____

4. Are you willing to pay the price—to stay in it for the long haul—in order to see your church become an equipping church? Why or why not?

_____

_____

more next-step
IDEAS

Use these practical ideas to help you become an empowering pastor serving in an equipping church:

1. **Preach a four- to six-week series on equipping.** Use passages such as Exodus 18 and 19; Romans 12; 1 Corinthians 12; Ephesians 4; and 1 Peter 2. You can find unedited messages from empowering pastors at www.rev.org: click on *Me to We* and then "Sermons."

2. **Look at your sermons** over the past month and see how many illustrations featured you "doing" ministry for others. Take special effort to avoid this in the future, and instead use illustrations featuring laypeople who are serving others.

3. **Do a church survey** to find out how many of your people are serving on a regular basis, both in the church and in the community. Find out what they are doing and how much time they're investing. Use this information as a benchmark to measure future growth and to affirm those who are impacting your community now.

4. **Write a one- to two-page ministry description for yourself,** each ministry leader in your church, and your board members. Discuss these with your leaders for input and editing. You can use samples provided at www.ChurchVolunteerCentral.com (click on "Tools" and "Ministry Descriptions").

5. **Read *Unfinished Business*** by Greg Ogden and consider using it for discussion among your leadership group or ad hoc dream team.

6. **Schedule a movie night** (don't forget the popcorn and refreshments!) with your staff and/or leadership team. Watch *The Preacher's Wife* and discuss these questions together after the movie:
   + How did this pastor's actions reveal a pastor-centric model of ministry?
   + How is our church similar in its approach to ministry?
   + How did this model of ministry adversely affect the pastor and his family?
   + How has this model of ministry adversely affected our church?
   + How can we avoid this approach to pastoring in our church? How might that help our church in the long run?

7. **Read *The Equipping Church*** by Sue Mallory and consider using it for discussion among your leadership group or ad hoc dream team.

8. **Plan a retreat.** Take a group of your most progressive influencers on an overnight retreat. Spend time together brainstorming how to move toward the equipping model in your church.

9. **Read *Partners in Ministry*** by James Garlow and consider using it for discussion among your leadership group or ad hoc dream team.

10. **Go to www.rev.org,** click on *Me to We* and then "Church of the Resurrection." Consider taking a group of people to their annual Leadership Institute, where they train and develop laypeople to serve in ministry.

11. **Read *Doing Church As a Team*** by Wayne Cordiero and consider using it for discussion among your leadership group or ad hoc dream team.

12. **Subscribe to Rev! Magazine** at a bulk rate, and use it to train, equip, and inspire your ministry leaders. Rev! is the only pastors' magazine designed as an equipping resource. Discuss key articles that apply to everyone as part of your leadership development plan. You can go to www.rev.org and click on "subscription center."

13. **Read *The Five Dysfunctions of a Team*** by Patrick Lencioni and consider using it for discussion among your leadership group or ad hoc dream team.

14. **Schedule a movie night** with your staff and/or leadership team and watch *Bruce Almighty*. Use these discussion questions:
    + Power is tempting. How can unhealthy power affect our ministry?
    + How does a pastor-centered, staff-centered approach to ministry tend to be power-oriented—even if it appears to be sacrificing?
    + What lessons did Bruce learn in this movie? How do those lessons relate to our church—what can we learn from them?

15. **Go to www.rev.org** and click on *Me to We* and then "Frazier Memorial Church" and consider taking a group of people to their annual *Every Member in Ministry Conference*, where they train and develop laypeople to serve in ministry.

16. **Read Exodus 18** as your personal devotional. How do you relate to Moses? What advice did Jethro give to help Moses take his ministry to a new level? How might this happen in your own ministry?

17. **Read Ephesians 4** as your personal devotional. How is this different from the way most pastors operate? How might spiritual maturity be connected to empowering others?

18. **Read Exodus 19 and 1 Peter 2** as your personal devotional. What is your role in developing the "priesthood of believers"? How is a pastor "one of them"? How is the role of the pastor unique among them?

19. **Schedule a movie night** with your staff and/or leadership team and watch *Luther*. Discuss these questions at the end:
    + What challenges did Luther face as he tried to do things differently in his ministry?
    + How might those challenges be similar to the challenges we'll face as we move our church toward an equipping model?
    + What inspiration did you find from Luther's example in this movie?

20. **Brainstorm service projects.** In your next ministry leadership meeting, come up with 10 possible service projects your church can do outside its walls. Discuss how to organize a one-day focus for serving individuals or community agencies.

21. **Read the story of Menlo Park Presbyterian Church's experiment.** They cancelled a weekend of worship services in order to have everyone in their church do various service projects in the community. Discuss the book with your leadership team. How feasible would this or something like it be in your church? (Go to www. rev.org, click on *Me to We* and then "Weekend of Service.")

22. **Look at your ministry calendar this week.** What ministry tasks could you do with an apprentice-in-training? Who could you invite to train for these tasks?

23. **Gather two to three people you trust fully,** and who you believe have a good sense of leadership. Discuss the most influential 5 percent of members in your church. Consider the spiritual maturity of these people and decide who might benefit from a six- to 12-month "pastor's group." During this group you'd disciple the participants in preparation for them to fill a leadership role in the church. Do the personal invitation, set the bar high, and make it a quality experience.

24. **Schedule a ministry fair!** Set aside a Sunday or weekend to help people discover what's going on in your church—and how they can get involved. Have each ministry set up a booth with details about the ministry, fun activities, snacks…and information on how to get involved.

25. **Read *The Externally Focused Church*** by Rick Rusaw and Eric Swanson, and consider using it for discussion among your leadership group or ad hoc dream team.

26. **Visit a church that models equipping.** For a partial list of churches and their Web sites, go to www.rev.org, and click on *Me to We* and then "Equipping Churches."

27. **Schedule a movie night** with your staff and/or leadership team and watch *Sister Act*. Don't forget popcorn and snacks! Use these questions to initiate a discussion:

- How did the "fortress mentality" of the church leaders affect the church's impact on its community?
- What were some of the struggles this parish experienced as it went through change?
- How is this church-change scenario like or unlike your situation?

28. **Go to www.ChurchVolunteerCentral.com** and click on "Pastors" in the drop-down menu under "Choose Your Ministry" to see what is there for you. Put it on your "favorites" list and visit regularly for free resources and materials.

29. **Visit the Externally Focused Church Network.** Go to www.rev.org and click on *Me to We* and then "Externally Focused Church Network" to find out what other churches are doing to impact their communities through service.

30. **Subscribe to the free, weekly e-newsletter,** Leadership Update, from Rev! Magazine, which has leadership insights and other church tips to help you develop your ministry leaders. Go to www.rev.org and click on "Leadership Update E-Newsletter."

31. **Schedule a movie night** with your staff and/or leadership team and watch *Ocean's Eleven*. More popcorn! Use these discussion questions:
- What different gifts did each character contribute in this movie?
- How did each character participate in the outcome?
- What tensions were evident in the movie? How are those similar to the tensions you'll face when you work together as a team?

32. **Read Mark 1 for your personal devotions.** What practices enabled Jesus to set priorities for his ministry? How do you think people felt about him when he didn't come to immediately fill their needs? Why is this both difficult and important to do as a local pastor?

33. **Consider having a consultant** work with your church or pastor's group to get a jump-start on this process. Go to www.ChurchVolunteerCentral.com and click on "Pastors" under the "Choose Your Ministry" drop-down menu, and then choose "Ask Your Consultant" under the "My Account" menu.

34. Try out equipping in your church's women's ministry. One of the best ways to reach women is through Girlfriends Unlimited, a growing network of churches helping women reach women through fun and interest-oriented relationships. For more info, go to www.rev.org, click on *Me to We* and then "Girlfriends Unlimited."

35. Communicate. Communication is important in equipping ministry, as is empowering your ministry leaders to connect quickly and conveniently. Consider Buzz Central, an integrated, Internet-hosted software that coordinates multiple facets of church communication and management. Go to www.rev.org, click on *Me to We* and then "Buzz Central."

36. Empower your church to serve. Kingdom Assignment is a great ministry begun by Pastor Denny and Leesa Bellesi. It invigorates people to think entrepreneurially as they find new ways to serve those in need around them. Find out more about this by going to www.rev.org, clicking on *Me to We* and then "Kingdom Assignment."

37. Equip your team with resources. To find more resource recommendations for your ministry leaders, go to www.rev.org, click on *Me to We* and then "Resource Recommends."

38. Read *The Five Star Church* by Alan Nelson and Stan Toler, and consider reading it as you strive to cast the vision for your new church paradigm.

For more **amazing resources**

visit us at
www.group.com...

...or call us at
1-800-747-6060 ext. 1370!

Group
Incredible things will happe